Happy Holidays
in Cross-Stitch™

Edited by *Vicki Blizzard and Barb Sprunger*

Happy Holidays
in Cross-Stitch™

Editors	Vicki Blizzard and Barb Sprunger
Art Director	Brad Snow
Publishing Services Manager	Brenda Gallmeyer
Assitant Art Director	Nick Pierce
Copy Supervisor	Michelle Beck
Copy Editors	Beverly Richardson and Judy Weatherford
Technical Editors	Marla Freeman and Elizabeth Spurlock
Graphic Arts Supervisor	Ronda Bechinski
Graphic Artist	Nicole Gage
Production Coordinator	Erin Augsburger
Production Assistants	Cheryl Kempf, Marj Morgan and Judy Neuenschwander
Photography	Tammy Christian, Don Clark, Matthew Owen and Jackie Schaffel
Photo Stylists	Tammy Nussbaum, Tammy M. Smith
Publishing Director	David J. McKee
Book Marketing Director	Dwight Seward
Editorial Director	Gary Richardson
Marketing Director	Dan Fink

TOLL-FREE ORDER LINE or to request a free catalog (800) 582-6643
Customer Service (800) 282-6643, **Fax** (800) 882-6643
Visit www.AnniesAttic.com

ISBN-10: 1-57367-240-8   ISBN-13: 978-1-57367-240-5   Library of Congress Control Number: 2006925195
Printed in the United States of America   First Printing: 2006   1 2 3 4 5 6 7 8 9

Introduction

Dear Cross-Stitch Friend,

Don't you just love holidays? If you're anything like us, you enjoy decorating your home with cross-stitch projects for each of them and are always looking for something new to stitch. "Have a project in progress at all times" is our motto, and we both have "at-home" projects as well as those we pack up and take along wherever we go.

We had so much fun selecting the delightful projects in this book with you in mind. We've included designs for Valentine's Day, St. Patrick's Day, Easter, Mother's and Father's Day, Fourth of July, Halloween (Vicki's favorite), Thanksgiving, and, of course, Christmas (Barb's favorite).

Because there were so many designs to choose from, we have added winter and birthday themes to this book, too.

Having all these beautiful projects in one book will keep you stitching for all of the holidays. We'll be stitching right along with you and will enjoy every minute—now we

just need to decide which one to start first!

Warm regards,

Vicki Barb

Vicki Blizzard &
Barb Sprunger

Table of Contents

Dance Hall
Revue

Original artwork by Susan Pisoni, adapted for cross-stitch by Mike Vickery

Dancing their way across a snowy glade, these cute little snow people will win your heart along the way!

Materials

- Lady blue 14-count Aida: 14 x 34 inches
- Kreinik blending filament: pearl #032

"Dance Hall Revue" was stitched on 14-count Aida by Zweigart using DMC floss.

Skill Level

**Average

Stitch Count

395 wide x 108 high

Approximate Design Size

11-count 36" x 9⅞"
14-count 28⅜" x 7¾"
16-count 24¾" x 6¾"
18-count 22" x 6"
22-count 18" x 5"
28-count over two threads 7" x 6½"

Instructions

1. Center and stitch design, using two strands floss or one strand floss and one strand blending filament for Cross-Stitch, and one strand floss for Backstitch. ❖

CROSS-STITCH (2X)

ANCHOR		DMC	COLORS
2	·	White	White
403	●	310	Black
119	✖	333	Very dark blue violet
977	?	334	Medium baby blue
236	⊞	413	Dark pewter gray
358	⋘	433	Medium brown
1046	a	435	Very light brown
57	▲	601	Dark cranberry
62	3	603	Cranberry
46	6	666	Bright red
305	⊞	725	Topaz
293	Y	727	Very light topaz
128	⟩	775	Very light baby blue
23	⌘	818	Baby pink
271	⁄	819	Light baby pink
229	↑	910	Dark emerald green
209	△	912	Light emerald green
204	~	913	Medium Nile green
316	⊕	970	Light pumpkin
905	✳	3031	Very dark mocha brown
129	n	3325	Light baby blue
167	e	3766	Light peacock blue
972	◆	3803	Dark mauve

KREINIK BLENDED CROSS-STITCH (2X)

ANCHOR		DMC	COLORS
2	⊗	White	White (1X) with 032 Pearl BF (1X)*

BACKSTITCH (1X)

ANCHOR		DMC	COLORS
360	—	3031	Very dark mocha brown*
167	—	3766	Light peacock blue

*Duplicate color

CROSS-STITCH (2X)

ANCHOR		DMC	COLORS
2	·	White	White
403	●	310	Black
119	✖	333	Very dark blue violet
977	?	334	Medium baby blue
236	#	413	Dark pewter gray
358	≪	433	Medium brown
1046	a	435	Very light brown
57	△	601	Dark cranberry
62	3	603	Cranberry
46	6	666	Bright red
305	▦	725	Topaz
293	Y	727	Very light topaz
128	>	775	Very light baby blue
23	⌘	818	Baby pink
271	/	819	Light baby pink
229	↑	910	Dark emerald green
209	△	912	Light emerald green
204	~	913	Medium Nile green
316	⊕	970	Light pumpkin
905	✳	3031	Very dark mocha brown
129	n	3325	Light baby blue
167	e	3766	Light peacock blue
972	◆	3803	Dark mauve

KREINIK BLENDED CROSS-STITCH (2X)

ANCHOR		DMC	COLORS
2	⊗	White	White (1X) with 032 Pearl BF (1X)*

BACKSTITCH (1X)

ANCHOR		DMC	COLORS
360	—	3031	Very dark mocha brown*
167	—	3766	Light peacock blue

*Duplicate color

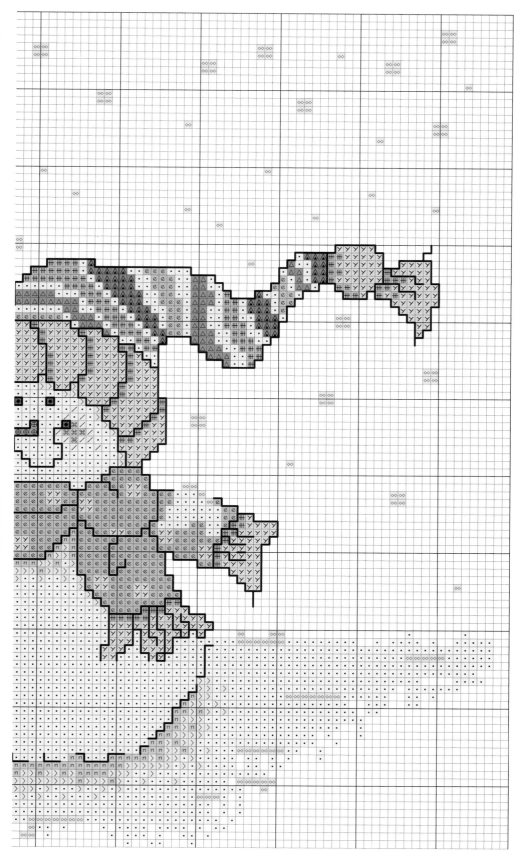

CROSS-STITCH (2X)

ANCHOR		DMC	COLORS
2	·	White	White
403	●	310	Black
119	✖	333	Very dark blue violet
977	?	334	Medium baby blue
236	#	413	Dark pewter gray
358	⋘	433	Medium brown
1046	a	435	Very light brown
57	▲	601	Dark cranberry
62	3	603	Cranberry
46	6	666	Bright red
305	⊞	725	Topaz
293	Y	727	Very light topaz
128	>	775	Very light baby blue
23	⌘	818	Baby pink
271	/	819	Light baby pink
229	♠	910	Dark emerald green
209	△	912	Light emerald green
204	~	913	Medium Nile green
316	⊕	970	Light pumpkin
905	✳	3031	Very dark mocha brown
129	n	3325	Light baby blue
167	e	3766	Light peacock blue
972	◆	3803	Dark mauve

KREINIK BLENDED CROSS-STITCH (2X)

ANCHOR		DMC	COLORS
2	∞	White	White (1X) with 032 Pearl BF (1X)*

BACKSTITCH (1X)

ANCHOR		DMC	COLORS
360	—	3031	Very dark mocha brown*
167	—	3766	Light peacock blue

*Duplicate color

Design by Pamela Kellogg

Softly shimmering stars and beaded icicles surround a snowflake frozen forevermore in crystal.

CROSS-STITCH (2X)

ANCHOR	DMC	COLOR
2	▣ White	White

EYELET STITCH (1X)

KREINIK #4 BRAID		COLOR
094	▬	Star blue

BACKSTITCH (2X)

ANCHOR	DMC	COLOR
2	▬ White	White*

ATTACH MILL HILL BEAD

MEDIUM BUGLE		COLOR
82010	▬	Ice, with white* (1X)
GLASS SEED		COLOR
00161	●	Crystal, with white* (1X)

ATTACH MILL HILL GLASS TREASURE

LARGE SNOWFLAKE		COLOR
12039	⬤	Crystal bright, with white* (1X)

*Duplicate color

Materials

- Ice blue 28-count Cashel linen: 11 x 13 inches
- Kreinik #4 very fine braid: star blue #094
- Mill Hill beads: ice #82010 medium bugle and crystal #00161 seed
- Mill Hill glass treasures charm: crystal bright #12039 large snowflake

"January Sampler" was stitched on 28-count ice blue Cashel linen by Zweigart using floss from DMC. Finished piece was custom framed.

Skill Level

***Advanced

Stitch Count

70 wide x 98 high

Approximate Design Size

11-count 6⅜" x 8⅞"
14-count 5" x 7"
16-count 4⅜" x 6⅛"
18-count 3⅞" x 5½"
22-count 3¼" x 4½"
28-count over two threads 5" x 7"

Instructions

1. Center and stitch design on 28-count Cashel linen, stitching over two threads using two strands floss for Cross-Stitch and Backstitch, and one strand very fine braid for Eyelet Stitch. Attach beads (see Bead Attachment Illustration on page 136) and charm as indicated on graph using one strand floss. ❖

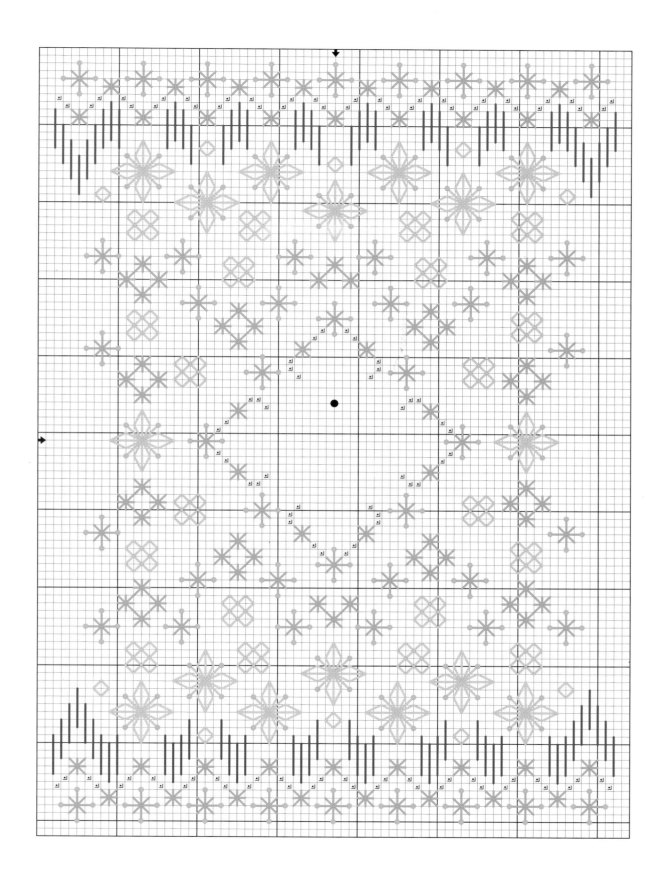

 # Winter's Eve

Design by Roberta Rankin

This serene landscape will remind faraway loved ones of the warmth and comfort of home.

Materials
- White 14-count Aida:
  10½ x 10½ inches

"Winter's Eve" was stitched on Wichelt 14-count Aida using DMC floss. Finished piece was custom framed.

Skill Level
**Average

Stitch Count
70 wide x 70 high

Approximate Design Size

11-count 6⅜" x 6⅜"
14-count 5" x 5"
16-count 4⅜" x 4⅜"
18-count 3⅞" x 3⅞"
22-count 3⅛" x 3⅛"

Instructions

1. Center and stitch design on 14-count Aida using three strands floss for Cross-Stitch and one strand floss for Backstitch. ❖

CROSS-STITCH (3X)

ANCHOR		DMC	COLORS
2	·	White	White
215	+	320	Medium pistachio green
9045	2	321	Red
1014	⊥	355	Dark terra cotta
5975	↓	356	Medium terra cotta
943	#	422	Light hazelnut brown
334	♥	606	Bright orange red
891	L	676	Light old gold
956	/	677	Very light old gold
256	4	704	Bright chartreuse
293	∞	727	Very light topaz
304	⁒	741	Medium tangerine
134	●	796	Dark royal blue
133	▲	797	Royal blue
134	★	820	Very dark royal blue
218	◢	890	Ultra dark pistachio green
205	I	911	Medium emerald green
848	↑	927	Light gray green
381	△	938	Ultra dark coffee brown
264	–	3348	Light yellow green
1032	✕	3752	Very light antique blue
1031	○	3753	Ultra very light antique blue

BACKSTITCH (1X)

ANCHOR		DMC	COLORS
1088	—	838	Very dark beige brown (walls)
218	—	890	Ultra dark pistachio green* (pine needles)
923	—	909	Very dark emerald green (shutters and door)
851	—	924	Very dark gray green (roofs)
1035	—	930	Dark antique blue (snow)
1015	—	3777	Very dark terra cotta (chimneys)

*Duplicate color

Snowflake Coasters

Designs by Mary B. Jones

Give these elegant coasters as a gift for the hard-to-shop-for person on your holiday list.

Materials

- Antique blue 14-count Aida: 2 (9 x 9-inch) pieces
- 2 square acrylic coasters

"Snowflake Coasters" were stitched on antique blue 14-count Aida from Charles Craft using DMC floss.

Skill Level

*Easy

Stitch Count

41 wide x 41 high

Approximate Design Size

11-count 3¾" x 3¾"
14-count 3" x 3"
16-count 2½" x 2½"
18-count 2¼" x 2¼"
22-count 1⅞" x 1⅞"

Instructions

1. Center and stitch design on 14-count Aida, using three strands floss for Cross-Stitch.

Finishing

1. Insert in acrylic coaster following manufacturer's instructions. ❖

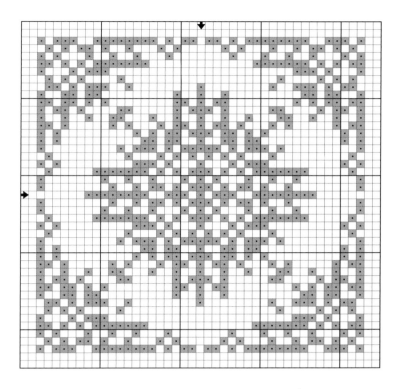

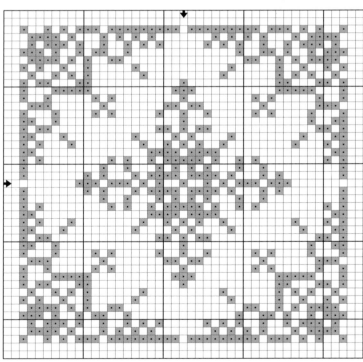

CROSS-STITCH (3X)

ANCHOR		DMC	COLOR
1	◼	B5200	Snow White

 # Winter Visitor

Design by Pamela Kellogg

This little robin stuck around during the winter to visit with his best snow friend.

Blending filament combined with the floss adds a touch of snow sparkle!

Materials

- Light blue 28-count Jobelan: 15 x 14½ inches
- Kreinik blending filament: pearl #032
- Kreinik #4 very fine braid: purple #012, fuchsia #024 and pearl #032

"Winter Visitor" was stitched on light blue 28-count Jobelan by Wichelt, using DMC floss. Finished piece was custom framed.

Skill Level

**Average

Stitch Count

98 wide x 92 high

Approximate Design Size

11-count 9" x 8⅜"
14-count 7" x 6½"
16-count 6⅛" x 5¾"
18-count 5⅜" x 5"
22-count 4½" x 4⅛"
28-count over two threads 7" x 6½"

Instructions

1. Center and stitch design, stitching over two threads using three strands floss or two strands floss and one strand blending filament for Cross-Stitch, three strands floss for French Knot, and one strand floss or #4 braid for Backstitch. ❖

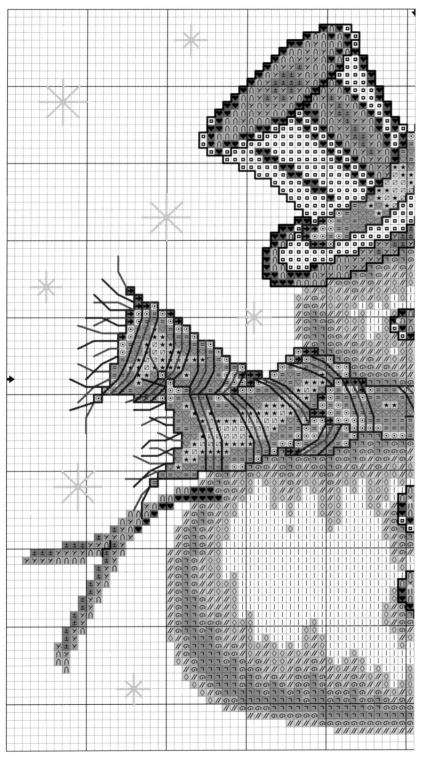

CROSS-STITCH (3X)

ANCHOR		DMC	COLORS
109	♡	209	Dark lavender
108	★	210	Medium lavender
342	☑	211	Light lavender
403	▫	310	Black
400	Y	317	Pewter gray
399	∩	318	Light steel gray
236	∩	413	Dark pewter gray
235	±	414	Dark steel gray
398	◪	415	Pearl gray
102	➜	550	Very dark violet
99	⊙	552	Medium violet
98	=	553	Violet
326	▣	720	Dark orange spice
925	╱	721	Medium orange spice
323	✕	722	Light orange spice
236	♥	3799	Very dark pewter gray
323	◁	3825	Pale pumpkin

KREINIK BLENDED CROSS-STITCH

ANCHOR		DMC	COLORS
2	☐	White	White (2X) with 032 pearl* BF (1X)
128	∥	775	Very light baby blue (2X) with 032 pearl* BF (1X)
129	˥	3325	Light baby blue (2X) with 032 pearl BF (1X)
1037	◇	3756	Ultra very light baby blue (2X) with 032 pearl* BF (1X)
9159	⌒	3841	Pale baby blue (2X) with 032 pearl* BF (1X)

BACKSTITCH (1X)

ANCHOR		DMC	COLORS
403	—	310	Black* (hat, bird, coal and eyes)
102	—	550	Very dark violet* (scarf and hatband)
326	—	720	Dark orange spice* (nose and bird)

KREINIK #4 BRAID		COLORS
012	—	Purple (scarf)
024	—	Fuchsia (scarf)
032	—	Pearl (snowflakes)

FRENCH KNOT (3X)

ANCHOR		DMC	COLOR
2	●	White	White* (eyes and buttons)

*Duplicate color

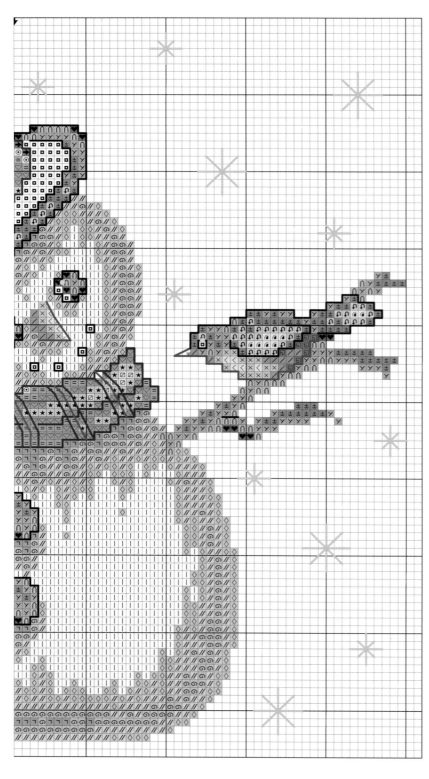

CROSS-STITCH (3X)

ANCHOR		DMC	COLORS
109	♡	209	Dark lavender
108	★	210	Medium lavender
342	☑	211	Light lavender
403	◘	310	Black
400	Y	317	Pewter gray
399	⋒	318	Light steel gray
236	⋒	413	Dark pewter gray
235	±	414	Dark steel gray
398	◪	415	Pearl gray
102	➜	550	Very dark violet
99	⊙	552	Medium violet
98	=	553	Violet
326	▣	720	Dark orange spice
925	／	721	Medium orange spice
323	✕	722	Light orange spice
236	♥	3799	Very dark pewter gray
323	◁	3825	Pale pumpkin

KREINIK BLENDED CROSS-STITCH

ANCHOR		DMC	COLORS
2	I	White	White (2X) with 032 pearl* BF (1X)
128	／／	775	Very light baby blue (2X) with 032 pearl* BF (1X)
129	⌐	3325	Light baby blue (2X) with 032 pearl BF (1X)
1037	◇	3756	Ultra very light baby blue (2X) with 032 pearl* BF (1X)
9159	⌐	3841	Pale baby blue (2X) with 032 pearl* BF (1X)

BACKSTITCH (1X)

ANCHOR		DMC	COLORS
403	—	310	Black* (hat, bird, coal and eyes)
102	—	550	Very dark violet* (scarf and hatband)
326	—	720	Dark orange spice* (nose and bird)
KREINIK #4 BRAID			COLORS
012	—		Purple (scarf)
024	—		Fuchsia (scarf)
032	—		Pearl (snowflakes)

FRENCH KNOT (3X)

ANCHOR		DMC	COLOR
2	●	White	White* (eyes and buttons)

*Duplicate color

God is Love,
and those who abide in Love
abide in God,
and God abides in them.

God is Love

Design by Vicki Schofield

Stitched on linen, interesting stitches add dimension and charm to this appealing piece.

Custom-cut mats display the stitching to its best advantage!

Materials

- Waterlily 28-count linen:
  15 x 12½ inches
- Kreinik #4 braid:
  gold hi luster #002HL
- DMC #9 pearl cotton: ecru
- Mill Hill glass seed beads:
  white #00479

"God Is Love" was stitched on water lily 28-count linen by Wichelt using silk mori milkpaint floss by Kreinik and #8 pearl cotton by DMC. Finished piece was custom framed.

Skill Level

***Advanced

Stitch Count

93 wide x 64 high

Approximate Design Size

11-count 8½" x 5⅞"
14-count 6⅝" x 4½"
16-count 5⅞" x 4"
18-count 5⅛" x 3½"
22-count 4¼" x 3"
28-count over two threads 6⅝" x 4½"

Instructions

1. Center and stitch design, stitching over two threads using two strands floss or one strand #4 braid for Cross-Stitch, and two strands for Straight Stitch. For Petite Stitch, stitch over one thread using one strand floss. Use one strand floss for Backstitch and for attaching beads. (See Bead Attachment Ilustration on page 136.)

2. Referring to Diagram A for Crown Stitch, use one strand #4 braid for vertical Backstitch inside curved stitch (shown in gold on diagram); use one strand #8 pearl cotton for remainder of stitch (Shown in gray on diagram).

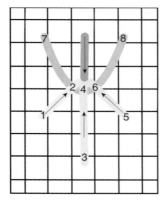

**Diagram A
Crown Stitch**

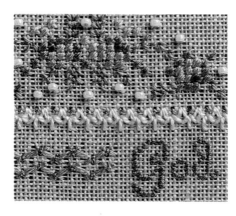

3. Referring to Diagram B for Tacked Herringbone Stitch, use two strands silk floss for Tacked Herringbone Stitch (shown in gray on diagram); use one strand #4 braid to tack with Backstitch (shown in gold on diagram). ❖

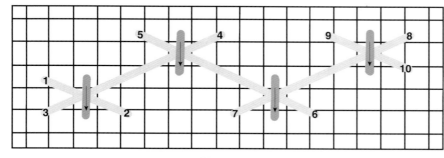

**Diagram B
Tacked Herringbone Stitch**

CROSS-STITCH (2X)

DMC		KREINIK SILK MORI MILK PAINT	COLORS
225	⌗	0113	Light Lenten rose
224	$	0114	Medium Lenten rose
316	%	0115	Dark Lenten rose
3726	••	0116	Very dark Lenten rose
524	+	0403	Light celadon
522	✳	0434	Medium moss green

CROSS-STITCH (1X)

KREINIK #4 BRAID		COLOR
002HL	☆	Gold hi luster

PETITE STITCH (1X)

DMC		KREINIK SILK MORI MILK PAINT	COLOR
522	▫	0434	Medium moss green*

STRAIGHT STITCH (2X)

DMC		KREINIK SILK MORI MILK PAINT	COLOR
224	—	0114	Medium Lenten rose*

TACKED HERRINGBONE STITCH (2X)

DMC		KREINIK SILK MORI MILK PAINT	COLOR
224	—	0114	Medium Lenten rose*

CROWN STITCH (1X)

DMC #8 PEARL COTTON		COLOR
Ecru	—	Ecru

BACKSTITCH (1X)

DMC		KREINIK SILK MORI MILK PAINT	COLOR
522	—	0434	Medium moss green*
KREINIK #4 BRAID			COLOR
002HL	—		Gold hi luster (for Crown and Tacked Herringbone stitches)

ATTACH MILL HILL BEAD

GLASS SEED		COLOR
00479	●	White, with 0403 light celadon* (1X)

*Duplicate color

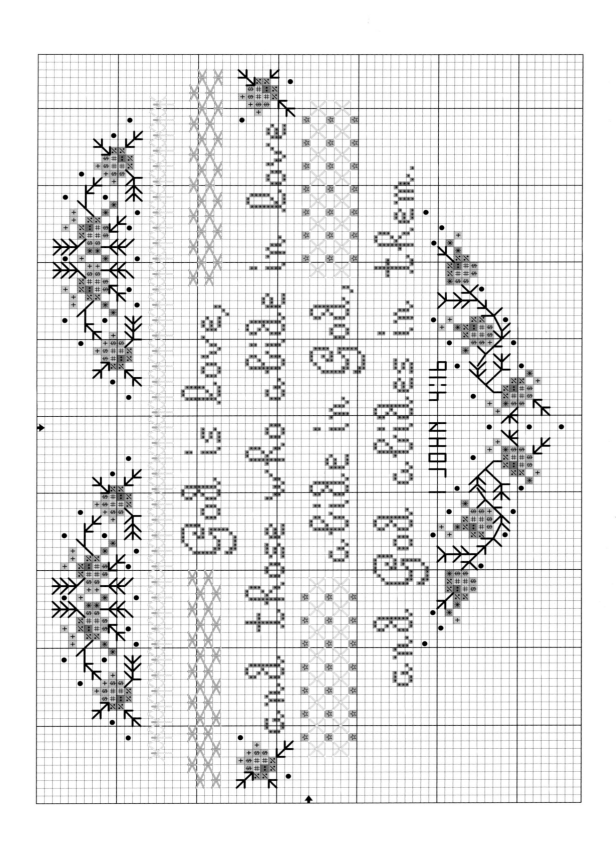

Design by Pamela Kellogg

Worked in rows, this sampler provides an ideal opportunity to practice a variety of stitches.

Smyrna Cross

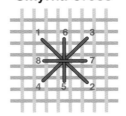

CROSS-STITCH (2X)

ANCHOR		DMC	COLORS
210	~	562	Medium jade
1028	■	3685	Very dark mauve
68	0	3687	Mauve
66	/	3688	Medium mauve
49	∷	3689	Light mauve
972	▽	3803	Dark mauve
KREINIK #4 BRAID			COLOR
032	⌘		Pearl

SMYRNA CROSS-STITCH (1X)

KREINIK #4 BRAID		COLOR
032	—	Pearl*

SATIN STITCH (3X)

ANCHOR		DMC	COLOR
66	—	3688	Medium mauve*

BACKSTITCH (1X)

ANCHOR		DMC	COLOR
212	—	561	Very dark jade

ATTACH MILL HILL BEAD

MEDIUM BUGLE		COLOR
82012	—	Royal plum, with DMC 3689/Anchor 49 light mauve* (1X)
GLASS SEED		COLOR
00479	●	White, with DMC 3689/Anchor 49 light mauve* (1X)

ATTACH MILL HILL GLASS TREASURE

MEDIUM FLUTED HEART		COLOR
12207	●	Matte ruby, with DMC 3685/Anchor 1028 dark mauve* (1X)

*Duplicate color

Materials

- Ice carnation 28-count Cashel Linen: 11 x 13 inches
- Kreinik #4 very fine braid: #032 pearl
- Mill Hill beads: royal plum #82012 medium bugle and white #00479 seed
- Mill Hill treasure: matte ruby #12207 medium fluted heart

"February Sampler" was stitched on ice carnation 28-count Cashel linen by Zweigart using floss from DMC. Finished piece was custom framed.

Skill Level

***Advanced

Stitch Count

70 wide x 98 high

Approximate Design Size

11-count 6⅜" x 9"
14-count 5" x 7"
16-count 4⅜" x 6⅛"
18-count 3⅞" x 5⅜"
22-count 3⅛" x 4⅜"
28-count over two threads 5" x 7"

Instructions

1. Center and stitch design on 28-count Cashel linen, stitching over two threads using three strands of floss for Satin Stitch, two strands of floss or very fine braid for Cross-Stitch, and one strand of floss for Backstitch. Use one strand very fine braid for Smyrna Cross-Stitch. Referring to graph for placement, attach treasure and beads (see Bead Attachment Illustration on page 136) using one strand floss. ❖

Busy bees will help keep your sewing room organized. Stitch them all or choose your favorite!

Sewing Bees

Designs by Ursula Michael

Materials

- White 28-count linen:
  14 x 16 inches (for Sewing Box)
  10 x 10 inches and 4 x 6 inches
  (for Scissors Keep)
  10 x 12 inches (for Pincushion)
  12 x 12 inches (for Safety Pin Keep
  and Notions Organizer)

- Kreinik #4 very fine braid: starburst #095 and steel gray #010HL
- Kreinik #1 Japan thread: Gold #002J
- Mill Hill Crayon seed beads: yellow #02059
- Mill Hill Glass Treasure: matte topaz #12204

- Oval sewing box with 6⅞ x 9¾-inch design area
- Oval pincushion with 2⅞ x 4½-inch design area
- Key rack with 5 x 7-inch design opening
- Yellow seed beads
- Glass bee charm

- 3 x 5-inch piece of mat board
- ¼ yard of fabric
- ½-inch button
- ⅔ yard of twisted cord
- 10-inch piece of yellow/white 4⅞-inch-wide 28-count linen stitchband
- Felt
- Ribbon:
  2 yards ³⁄₁₆-inch-wide
  ⅓ yard ½-inch-wide
- 5-inch square of foam core board

"Sewing Bees" projects were stitched on 28-count Linen and 28-count Stitchband by Zweigart, using DMC floss. Large Oval Shaker Sewing Box with handle, Oval Pincushion and Key Rack shown are by Sudberry House.

Skill Level
**Average

Notions Organizer
Stitch Count
76 wide x 60 high

Approximate Design Size
11-count 7" x 5½"
14-count 5½" x 4⅜"
16-count 4¾" x 3¾"
18-count 4¼" x 3⅜"
22-count 3½" x 2¾"
28-count over two threads 5½" x 4⅜"

Instructions
1. Center and stitch design, stitching over two threads and using three strands floss or two strands very fine braid for Cross-Stitch. Use one strand very fine braid for Backstitch.

2. Position and secure design in key rack frame following manufacturer's instructions.

Needle Roll
Stitch Count
81 wide x 34 high

Approxmate Design Size
11-count 7⅛" x 3⅛"
14-count 5⅞" x 2½"
16-count 5⅛" x 2⅛"
18-count 4½" x 2"

22-count 3¾" x 1⅝"
28-count over two threads 5⅞" x 2½"

Instructions
1. Center and stitch design, stitching over two threads and using three strands floss or two strands very fine braid for Cross-Stitch. Use two strands floss or one strand very fine braid for Backstitch. Use one strand coordinating floss for securing beads.

2. At each end of design, fold under ½ inch; press. Fold ½ inch again and sew close to first fold.

3. Cut two 18-inch-long pieces of ³⁄₁₆-inch-wide ribbon. Cut 3 x 6-inch piece from felt.

4. For ties, sew center of one ribbon to hemmed edge ¼ inch from each decorative edge.

5. Center and sew felt to wrong side of design. Store needles in felt; begin at end without ties and roll up, tie to secure.

Scissors Keep
Stitch Count
28 wide x 28 high

Approximate Design Size
11-count 2⅝" x 2⅝"
14-count 2" x 2"
16-count 1¾" x 1¾"
18-count 1⅝" x 1⅝"
22-count 1⅜" x 1⅜"
28-count over two threads 2" x 2"

Instructions
1. Center and stitch design on 10 x 10-inch piece of Linen, stitching over two threads and using three strands floss for Cross-Stitch. Use two strands floss or one strand Japan thread for Backstitch. Use two strands coordinating floss for securing glass treasure.

2. Trim design to 4 inches square.

3. From fabric, cut one 4-inch-square piece for front and one 4 x 6-inch piece for back. From ³⁄₁₆-inch ribbon, cut one 24-inch piece. Use ½-inch seams.

4. For front, with right sides together and leaving a small opening for turning, sew design and 4-inch-square fabric piece together. Turn right sides out; sew opening closed.

5. For back, with right sides together and leaving one side open for turning, sew 4 x 6-inch piece of fabric and 4 x 6-inch piece of linen together; turn right sides out. Insert mat board; sew open side closed.

6. With design on top, hold front and back together matching bottom edges; sew together leaving top edge of design open to form pocket.

7. Sew twisted cord around edge as shown in photo.

8. Secure one end of ribbon to upper left corner of back with button.

9. Tie remaining end of ribbon to scissors; store scissors in pocket when not in use.

Safety Pin Keep
Stitch Count
50 wide x 50 high

Approximate Design Size
11-count 4⅝" x 4⅝"
14-count 3⅝" x 3⅝"
16-count 3⅛" x 3⅛"
18-count 2⅞" x 2⅞"
22-count 2⅜" x 2⅜"
28-count over two threads 3⅝" x 3⅝"

Instructions
1. Center and stitch design, stitching

over two threads and using three strands floss or two strands very fine braid for Cross-Stitch. Use two strands floss or one strand very fine braid for Backstitch. Use one strand coordinating floss for securing beads.

2. Trim design to 5 inches square.

3. Cut 4-inch-square piece from felt.

4. Position and mount design to foam core board. Fold 2-inch-wide ribbon in half. Lay ribbon along back of design with fold 2 inches above top of design. Glue felt to back of design over ribbon. Trim ribbon ends at an angle.

Pincushion
Stitch Count
51 wide x 32 high

Approximate Design Size
11-count 4⅝" x 3"
14-count 3¾" x 2⅜"
16-count 3¼" x 2"
18-count 2⅞" x 1⅞"
22-count 2⅜" x 1½"
28-count over two threads 3¾" x 2⅜"

Instructions
1. Center and stitch design, stitching over two threads and using three strands floss or two strands very fine braid or two strands Japan thread for Cross-Stitch. Use two strands floss or one strand very fine braid for Backstitch.

2. Position and secure design in pincushion following manufacturer's instructions.

Sewing Box
Stitch Count
120 wide x 90 high

Approximate Design Size
11-count 11" x 8¼"
14-count 8⅝" x 6 ½"
16-count 7½" x 5⅝"
18-count 6¾" x 5"
22-count 5½" x 4⅛"
28-count over two threads 8⅝" x 6½"

Instructions
1. Center and stitch design, stitching over two threads and using three strands floss or two strands very fine braid for Cross-Stitch. Use two strands floss or one strand very fine braid for Backstitch. Use one strand coordinating floss for securing beads (see Bead Attachment Illustration on page 136).

2. Position and secure design in box top following manufacturer's instructions. ❖

Notions Organizer

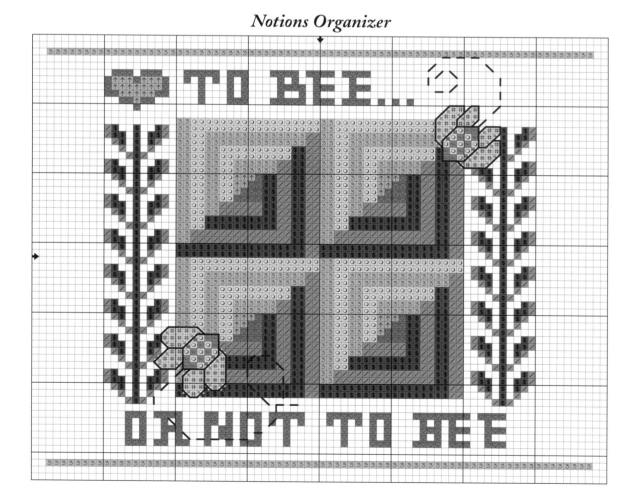

Needle Roll

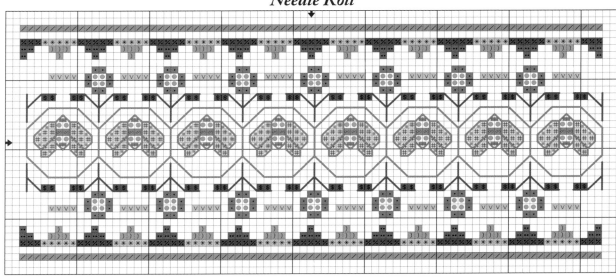

Notions Organizer

CROSS-STITCH (3X)

ANCHOR		DMC	COLORS
895	↑	223	Light shell pink
403	∞	310	Black
218	$	319	Very dark pistachio green
295	◯	726	Light topaz
242	╱	989	Forest green
896	♥	3721	Very dark shell pink
306	3	3820	Dark straw

CROSS STITCH (2X)

KREINIK #4 BRAID		COLOR
	#	095	Starburst

BACKSTITCH (1X)

KREINIK #4 BRAID		COLOR
010HL	—	Steel gray

Scissors Keep

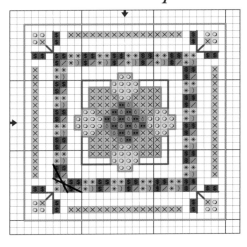

Scissors Keep

CROSS-STITCH (3X)

ANCHOR		DMC	COLORS
218	$	319	Very dark pistachio green
978	)	322	Dark baby blue
310	••	434	Light brown
1045	△	436	Tan
295	◯	726	Light topaz
298	✕	972	Deep canary
242	╱	989	Forest green
140	✳	3755	Baby blue

BACKSTITCH (2X)

ANCHOR		DMC	COLOR
218	—	319	Very dark pistachio green*

BACKSTITCH (1X)

KREINIK #1 JAPAN THREAD		COLOR
002J	—	Gold #1

ATTACH MILL HILL GLASS TREASURE

BEE		COLOR
12204	—	Matte topaz, with DMC 726 light topaz* (1X)

*Duplicate color

Needle Roll

CROSS-STITCH (3X)

ANCHOR		DMC	COLORS
403	∞	310	Black
218	$	319	Very dark pistachio green
978	)	322	Dark dark baby blue
310	••	434	Light brown
1039	■	518	Light wedgewood
359	╱	801	Dark coffee brown
242	╱	989	Forest green
140	✳	3755	Baby blue
928	V	3761	Light sky blue

CROSS-STITCH (1X)

KREINIK #4 BRAID		COLOR
095	#	Starburst

BACKSTITCH (1X)

ANCHOR		DMC	COLOR
218	—	319	Very dark pistachio green*

BACKSTITCH (1X)

KREINIK #4 BRAID		COLOR
010HL	—	Steel gray

ATTACH MILL HILL BEADS

CRAYON SEED		COLOR
02059	●	Yellow

*Duplicate color

Safety Pin Keep

CROSS-STITCH (3X)

ANCHOR		DMC	COLORS
403	⊗	310	Black
218	$	319	Very dark pistachio green
310	••	434	Light brown
1045	◊	436	Tan
1039	•	518	Light wedgewood
295	O	726	Light topaz
361	L	738	Very light tan
242	/	989	Forest green
896	♡	3721	Dark shell pink
928	V	3761	Light sky blue

CROSS-STITCH (2X)

KREINIK #4 BRAID		COLOR
095	⊞	Starburst

BACKSTITCH (2X)

ANCHOR		DMC	COLORS
403	—	310	Black* (lettering and beehive)
218	—	319	Very dark pistachio green* (vines)
1039	—	518	Light wedgewood* (inside border)
896	—	3721	Dark shell pink* (heart)

BACKSTITCH (1X)

KREINIK #4 BRAID		COLOR
010HL	—	Steel gray* (bees and trail)

ATTACH MILL HILL BEADS

CRAYON SEED		COLOR
02059	●	Yellow

*Duplicate color

Pincushion

CROSS-STITCH (3X)

ANCHOR		DMC	COLORS
895	↑	223	Light shell pink
893	6	224	Very light shell pink
403	⊗	310	Black
398	◨	415	Pearl gray
860	+	522	Fern green
858	a	524	Very light fern green
901	◆	680	Dark old gold
293	√	727	Very light topaz

CROSS-STITCH (2X)

KREINIK #4 BRAID		COLOR
095	⊞	Starburst
KREINIK #1 JAPAN THREAD		COLOR
002J	∅	Gold

BACKSTITCH (2X)

ANCHOR		DMC	COLOR
403	—	310	Black*

BACKSTITCH (1X)

KREINIK #4 BRAID		COLOR
010HL	—	Steel gray

*Duplicate color

Sewing Box

CROSS-STITCH (3X)

ANCHOR		DMC	COLORS
895	↑	223	Light shell pink
403	⊗	310	Black
218	$	319	Very dark pistachio green
978	)	322	Dark baby blue
310	••	434	Light brown
1045	◊	436	Tan
1039	•	518	Light wedgewood
361	L	738	Very light tan
158	2	747	Very light sky blue
359	▨	801	Dark coffee brown
242	/	989	Forest green
896	♡	3721	Dark shell pink
1040	✳	3755	Baby blue

CROSS-STITCH (2X)

KREINIK #4 BRAID		COLORS
095	⊞	Starburst
101HL	—	Steel gray

BACKSTITCH (2X)

ANCHOR		DMC	COLORS
403	—	310	Black*
218	—	319	Very dark pistachio green*

BACKSTITCH (1X)

KREINIK #4 BRAID		COLOR
101HL	—	Steel gray*

ATTACH MILL HILL BEADS

CRAYON SEED		COLOR
02059	●	Yellow

*Duplicate color

Safety Pin Keep

Pincushion

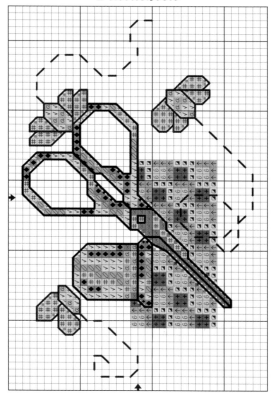

Sewing Box

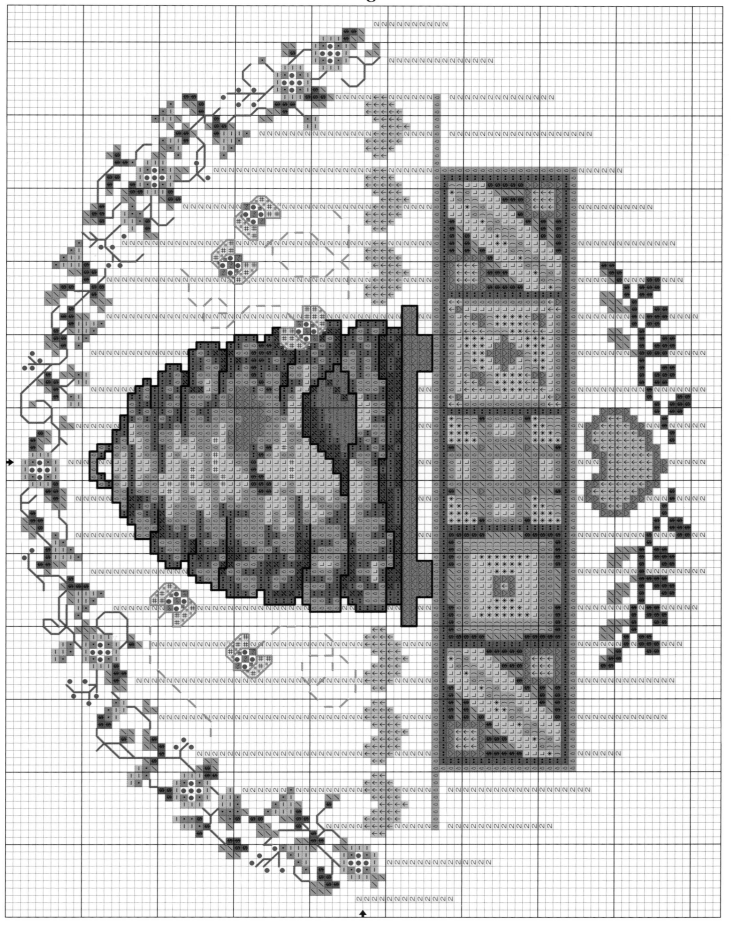

Hearts & Flowers

Design by Pamela Kellogg

Bursting with heartfelt romance, this pair is perfect to display in a feminine bedroom.

Materials (for each)
- White 14-count Aida:
  10½ x 10½ inches
- Kreinik blending filament:
  star pink #092

"Hearts & Flowers" was stitched on 14-count Aida by Wichelt using DMC floss. Finished pieces were custom framed.

Skill Level
**Average

Stitch Count
70 wide x 80 high

Approximate Design Size
11-count 6⅜" x 7¼"
14-count 5" x 5 ¾"
16-count 4⅜" x 5"
18-count 3⅞" x 4⅜"
22-count 3⅛" x 3⅝"

Instructions
1. Center and stitch design on fabric, using two strands floss or two strands floss and one strand blending filament for Cross-Stitch, and one strand floss for Backstitch. ❖

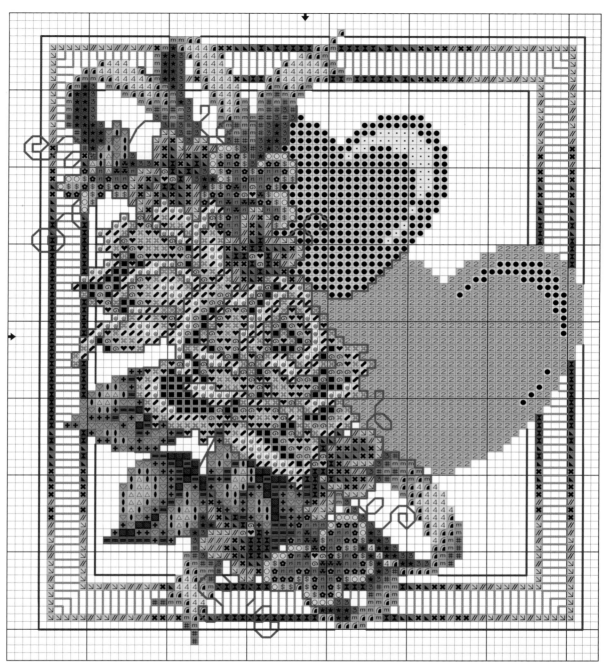

Hearts & Roses

CROSS-STITCH (2X)

ANCHOR		DMC	COLORS
109	✿	209	Dark lavender
108	$	210	Medium lavender
342	○	211	Light lavender
218	▬	319	Very dark pistachio green
215	♡	320	Medium pistachio green
119	✖	333	Very dark blue violet
118	✖	340	Medium blue violet
117	//	341	Light blue violet
217	+	367	Dark pistachio green
214	◖	368	Light pistachio green
213	△	369	Very light pistachio green
99	✤	552	Medium violet

98	n	553	Violet
1064	m	597	Turquoise
1062	◠	598	Light turquoise
275	◎	746	Off-white
307	■	783	Medium topaz
218	◣	890	Ultra dark pistachio green
292	◢	3078	Very light golden yellow
1030	◤	3746	Dark blue violet
120	↘	3747	Very light blue violet
1068	★	3808	Ultra very dark turquoise
1066	3	3809	Very dark turquoise
1066	#	3810	Dark turquoise
1060	4	3811	Very light turquoise
306	◔	3820	Dark straw
305	♥	3821	Straw
295	⌘	3822	Light straw

KREINIK BLENDED CROSS STITCH

ANCHOR		DMC	COLORS
24	●	776	Medium pink (2x) with 092 star pink BF (1X)
23	·	818	Baby pink (2x) with 092 star pink BF (1X)
36	2	3326	Light rose (2x) with 092 star pink BF (1X)

BACKSTITCH (1X)

ANCHOR		DMC	COLORS
119	—	333	Very dark blue violet* (outside border)
381	—	938	Ultra dark coffee brown (all other)
120	—	3747	Very light blue violet* (inside border)

*Duplicate color

Hearts & Pansies

CROSS-STITCH (2X)

ANCHOR		DMC	COLORS
2	I	White	White
109	✿	209	Dark lavender
108	$	210	Medium lavender
342	O	211	Light lavender
399	☆	318	Light steel gray
218	=	319	Very dark pistachio green
215	♡	320	Medium pistachio green
119	X	333	Very dark blue violet
118	✖	340	Medium blue violet
117	//	341	Light blue violet
217	+	367	Dark pistachio green
214	❙	368	Light pistachio green
213	△	369	Very light pistachio green
235	◕	414	Dark steel gray
398	◓	415	Pearl gray
99	✺	552	Medium violet
98	n	553	Violet
1064	m	597	Turquoise
1062	◖	598	Light turquoise
234	Z	762	Very light pearl gray
307	■	783	Medium topaz
218	◩	890	Ultra dark pistachio green
381	◆	938	Ultra dark coffee brown
292	/	3078	Very light golden yellow
1030	◣	3746	Dark blue violet
120	◥	3747	Very light blue violet
1068	★	3808	Ultra very dark turquoise
1066	3	3809	Very dark turquoise
1066	#	3810	Dark turquoise
1060	4	3811	Very light turquoise
306	☝	3820	Dark straw
305	♥	3821	Straw
295	⌘	3822	Light Straw

KREINIK BLENDED CROSS STITCH

ANCHOR		DMC	COLORS
24	●	776	Medium pink (2x) with 092 star pink BF (1X)
23	·	818	Baby pink (2x) with 092 star pink BF (1X)
36	2	3326	Light rose (2x) with 092 star pink BF (1X)

BACKSTITCH (1X)

ANCHOR		DMC	COLORS
119	—	333	Very dark blue violet* (outside border)
381	—	938	Ultra dark coffee brown* (all other)
120	—	3747	Very light blue violet* (inside border)

*Duplicate color

Design by Patricia Maloney Martin

Here's an excuse to eat chocolate—the shamrock wreath is too pretty to keep covered with candy!

CROSS-STITCH (3X)

ANCHOR		DMC	COLORS
215	◆	320	Medium pistachio green
6	⌒	353	Peach
290	✿	444	Dark lemon
256	⌘	704	Bright chartreuse

BACKSTITCH (2X)

ANCHOR		DMC	COLORS
215	—	320	Medium pistachio green* (shamrocks, lettering)
381	—	938	Ultra dark coffee brown (blossoms)

FRENCH KNOT (2X)

ANCHOR		DMC	COLORS
215	●	320	Medium pistachio green*
290	○	444	Dark lemon*

*Duplicate color

Materials
- White 14-count Aida: 9 x 9 inches
- 6-inch-round coaster/candy dish with 5-inch design area

"Irish Blessing" was stitched on white 14-count Aida by Zweigart using DMC floss. Finished piece is displayed in #15801 Coaster/Candydish from Sudberry House.

Skill Level
**Average

Stitch Count
43 wide x 39 high

Approximate Design Size
11-count 4" x 3½"
14-count 3" x 2¾"
16-count 2⅝" x 2⅜"
18-count 2⅜" x 2⅛"
22-count 2" x 1¾"

Instructions
1. Center and stitch design on 14-count Aida, using three strands floss for Cross-Stitch and two strands floss for Backstitch and French knot.

Finishing
1. Place stitched design in coaster/candy dish following manufacturer's instructions. ❖

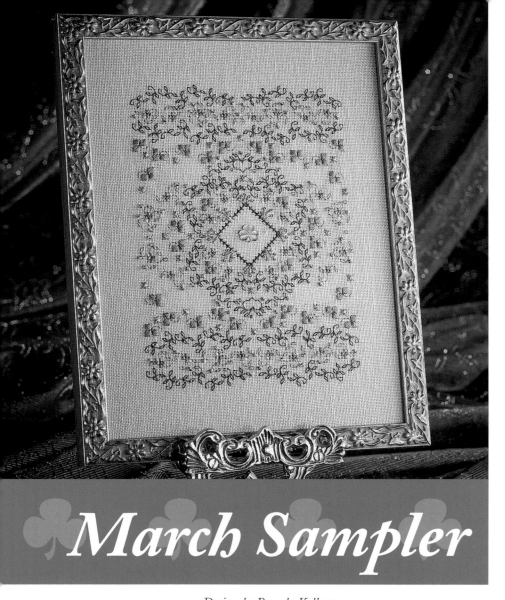

CROSS-STITCH (2X)

ANCHOR		DMC	COLORS
218	■	319	Very dark pistachio green
215	◩	320	Medium pistachio green
119	♥	333	Very dark blue violet
118	⬚	340	Medium blue violet
1020	★	3747	Very light blue violet

SMYRNA CROSS-STITCH (1X)

KREINIK #4 BRAID		COLOR
002	—	Gold

SATIN STITCH (3X)

ANCHOR		DMC	COLOR
215	—	320	Medium pistachio green*

STRAIGHT STITCH (1X)

KREINIK #4 BRAID		COLOR
002	—	Gold*

BACKSTITCH (1X)

ANCHOR		DMC	COLORS
218	—	319	Very dark pistachio green*
215	—	320	Medium pistachio green*
KREINIK #4 BRAID	—		COLOR Gold*
002	—		

ATTACH MILL HILL BEAD

GLASS SEED		COLOR
00252	●	Iris, with Anchor 1042/DMC 504 very light blue green (1X)
PETITE GLASS		COLOR
40557	●	Gold, with Anchor 1042/DMC 504 very light blue green* (1X)

ATTACH MILL HILL GLASS TREASURE

SHAMROCK		COLOR
12145	●	Matte emerald, with Anchor 1042/DMC 504 very light blue green* (1X)

*Duplicate color

Smyrna Cross

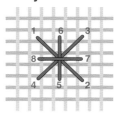

March Sampler

Design by Pamela Kellogg

Celebrate the coming of spring and St. Paddy's Day

with delicate flowers and shamrocks.

Materials

- Mint green 28-count Cashel linen: 11 x 13 inches
- Kreinik #4 very fine braid: gold #002
- Mill Hill beads: iris #00252 glass seed and gold #40557 petite glass seed
- Mill Hill glass treasures charm: matte emerald #12145 shamrock

"March Sampler" was stitched on mint green 28-count Cashel linen by Zweigart using DMC floss. Finished piece was custom framed.

Skill Level

***Advanced

Stitch Count

70 wide x 98 high

Approximate Design Size

11-count 6⅜" x 8⅞"
14-count 5" x 7"
16-count 4⅜" x 6⅛"
18-count 3⅞" x 5½"
22-count 3¼" x 4½"
28-count over two threads 5" x 7"

Instructions

1. Center and stitch design on 28-count Cashel linen, stitching over two threads using two strands floss for Cross-Stitch, three strands floss for Satin Stitch, one strand very fine braid for Smyrna Cross-Stitch and Straight Stitch, and one strand of floss for Backstitch.

2. Attach beads (see Bead Attachment illustration on page 136) and glass treasure as indicated on graph using one strand of floss. ❖

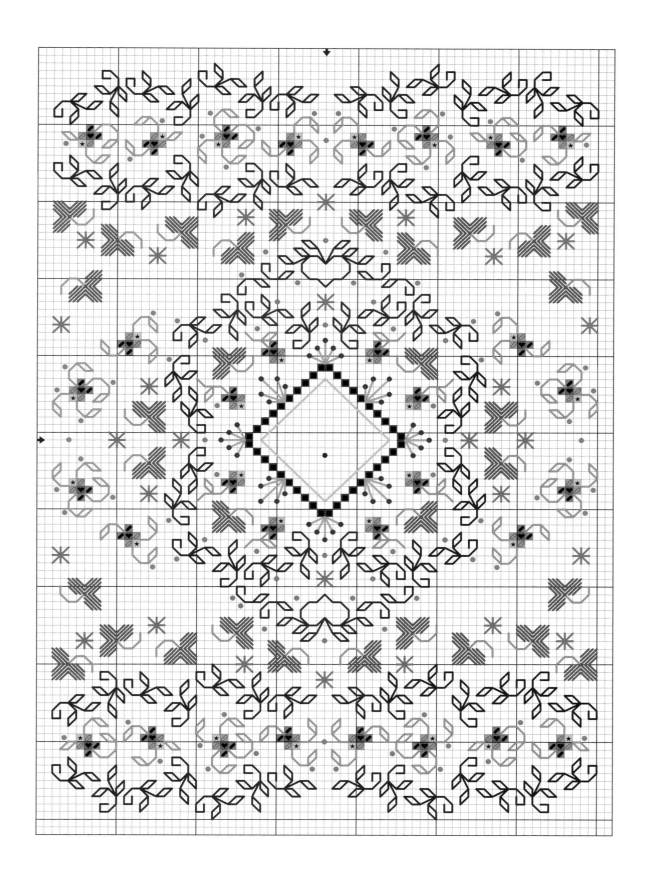

Celtic Sachets

Designs by Susan Stadler

Easy backstitching creates intricately interwoven Celtic patterns

that grace the fronts of these feminine sachets.

Materials

- 28-count Cashel linen:
  4½ x 12 inches apricot
  (for Celtic Knot)
  4½ x 12 inches carnation pink
  (for Heart Knot)
  4½ x 12 inches mint green
  (for Fantasy Knot)
- 2 (5-inch) lengths ¾-inch-wide lace trim (for each sachet)
- 2 (18-inch) lengths ⅛-inch-wide ribbon in two coordinating colors (for each sachet)
- Potpourri

"Celtic Sachets" were stitched on 28-count Cashel linen from Zweigart using Eterna Silk Overdyed MiniTwist floss from Yodamo Inc.

Skill Level

*Easy

Stitch Count

28 wide x 28 high (each)

Approximate Design Size

11-count 2⅝" x 2⅝"
14-count 2" x 2"
16-count 1¾" x 1¾"
18-count 1⅝" x 1⅝"
22-count 1¼" x 1¼"
28-count over two threads 2" x 2"

Instructions

Note: Begin stitching with left uppermost corner 3¼ inches down from top edge and 1¼ inches in from left edge of fabric.

1. Center and stitch design on linen, stitching over two threads using two strands floss for Backstitch.

Finishing

1. Turn under a ¼-inch hem on raw edges of narrow ends. On right side of piece, machine stitch lace trim across narrow ends, catching hem in stitching.

2. Fold linen piece in half with right sides together, matching hemmed narrow edges; sew side seams, using ½-inch seam allowance. Trim seams and corners; turn right side out.

3. Fill sachet with potpourri to within 2½ inches of top; tie ribbons in a bow around sachet to close. ❖

Celtic Knot

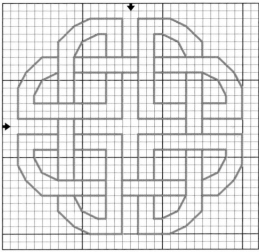

Fantasy Knot

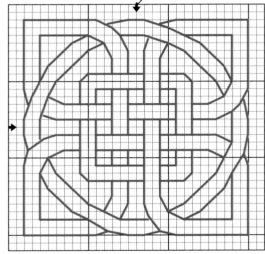

Heart Knot

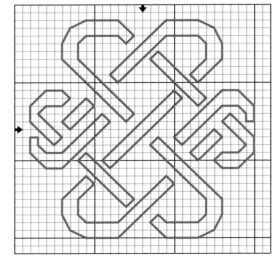

BACKSTITCH (2X)

DMC		ETERNA SILK COLORS
911	—	Rain forest (Fantasy Knot)
309	—	Marionberries (Heart Knot)
721	—	Carrot (Celtic Knot)

Easter Memories

Design by C.M. Barr

These vintage-look bunnies are gathered around the basket to wish you the happiest of Easters!

Materials
- Baby lotion 28-count Lugana: 9½ x 9 inches

"Easter Memories" was stitched on baby lotion 28-count Lugana by Zweigart using DMC floss. Finished piece was custom framed.

Skill Level
**Average

Stitch Count
53 wide x 46 high

Approximate Design Size
11-count 4⅞" x 4⅛"
14-count 3¾" x 3¼"
16-count 3⅜" x 2⅞"
18-count 3" x 2½"
22-count 2⅜" x 2"

Instructions
1. Center and stitch design on 28-count Lugana, stitching over two threads using three strands floss for Cross-Stitch and one strand floss for Backstitch. ❖

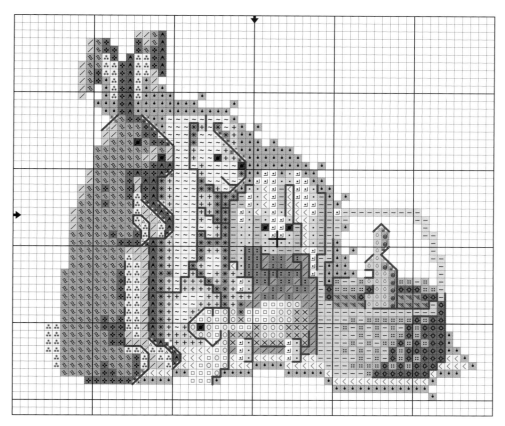

CROSS-STITCH (3X)

ANCHOR		DMC	COLORS
387	◢	Ecru	Ecru
895	✳	223	Light shell pink
893	+	224	Very light shell pink
1026	~	225	Ultra very light shell pink
358	✿	433	Medium brown
310	∷	434	Light brown
1045	−	436	Tan
860	◣	522	Fern green
401	<	535	Very light ash gray
898	◪	611	Drab brown
832	◇	612	Light drab brown
903	◆	640	Very dark beige gray
392	−	642	Dark beige gray
830	·	644	Medium beige gray
891	✕	676	Light old gold

ANCHOR		DMC	COLORS
301	○	744	Pale yellow
1088	▲	838	Very dark beige brown
1086	✸	839	Dark beige brown
1084	◥	840	Medium beige brown
1082	∕	841	Light beige brown
1080	✲	842	Very light beige brown
850	∕	926	Medium gray green
848	∷	927	Light gray green
392	□	3078	Very light golden yellow
382	◼	3371	Black brown

BACKSTITCH (1X)

ANCHOR	DMC	COLORS
905	—	3021	Very dark brown gray (bunnies, basket)
382	—	3371	Black brown* (bunny nose)

*Duplicate color

Easter Eggs

Designs by Mike Vickery

Stitch up these five festive eggs to adorn your Easter tree—shiny braids

create the effect of sunlight and shadows.

Materials

- White 14-count plastic canvas
- Kreinik #8 fine braid: pearl #032, pale yellow #191, sunlight #9100, star green #9194, blossom #9200 and periwinkle #9294
- Kreinik #4 very fine braid: pearl #032
- White felt
- Fabric glue

"Easter Eggs" were stitched on white 14-count plastic canvas using DMC floss.

Skill Level

*Easy

Stitch Count

19 wide x 25 high (each)

Approximate Design Size

11-count 1¾" x 2¼"
14-count 1⅜" x 1¾"
16-count 1⅛" x 1½"
18-count 1" x 1⅜"
22-count ⅞" x 1⅛"

Instructions

1. Stitch designs on plastic canvas, using three strands floss or one strand #8 fine braid for Cross-Stitch, and one strand #4 very fine braid for Backstitch.

Finishing

1. Trim plastic canvas one hole beyond stitching.

2. For each egg, cut an 8-inch length of braid; glue both ends to top back of egg to form a hanging loop.

3. Glue back of each egg to white felt; let dry. Trim felt to fit ornament. ❖

CROSS-STITCH (3X)

ANCHOR		DMC	COLORS
118	○	340	Medium blue violet
98	=	553	Violet
305	◉	725	Topaz
275	∷	746	Off-white
209	∧	912	Light emerald green
75	♡	962	Medium dusty rose
1037	+	3756	Ultra very light baby blue

CROSS-STITCH (1X)

KREINIK #8 BRAID		COLORS
032	⏎	Pearl
191	⏚	Pale yellow
9100	☆	Sunlight
9194	∞	Star green
9200	◿	Blossom
9294	Y	Periwinkle

BACKSTITCH (1X)

KREINIK #4 BRAID		COLOR
032	—	Pearl

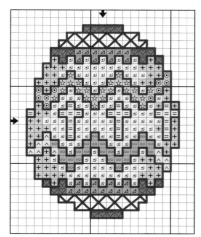

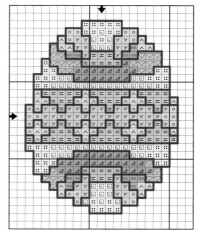

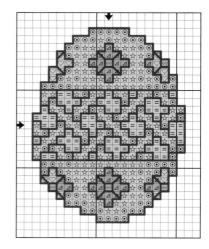

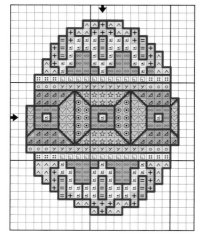

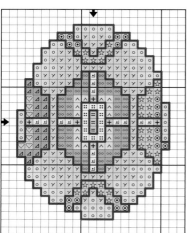

Happy Easter

Design by Barbara Sestok

Lazy-Daisy and Straight Stitches add interest to the bright spring colors of this pretty blue Easter egg.

Lazy-Daisy Stitch

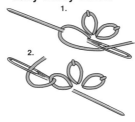

Materials
- Miracle mint 25-count Lugana: 14 x 14 inches

"Happy Easter" was stitched on miracle mint 25-count Lugana by Zweigart using DMC floss. Finished piece was custom framed.

Skill Level
**Average

Stitch Count
64 wide x 64 high

Approximate Design Size
11-count 5⅞" x 5⅞"
14-count 4½" x 4½"
16-count 4" x 4"
18-count 3½" x 3½"
22-count 3" x 3"
25-count over two threads 5" x 5"

Instructions
1. Center and stitch design, stitching over two threads and using three strands floss for Cross-Stitch and Straight Stitch. Use two strands floss for Backstitch designated by color key. Use one strand floss for all remaining Backstitch.

2. Use two strands floss for medium pistachio green and light blue Lazy-Daisy Stitch and three strands floss for white Lazy-Daisy Stitch

3. Use two strands floss for French Knots. French Knots in dark straw are wrapped three times. French Knots in very light plum and medium pistachio green are wrapped twice. ❖

CROSS-STITCH (3X)

ANCHOR		DMC	COLORS
2	⋅	White	White
216	◣	163	Medium celadon green
108	∷	210	Medium lavender
215	=	320	Medium pistachio green
118	Z	340	Medium blue violet
214	△	368	Light pistachio green
1043	••	369	Very light pistachio green
288	I	445	Light lemon
253	◪	472	Ultra light avocado green
98	✳	553	Violet
295	✓	726	Light topaz
161	L	813	Light blue
160	↑	827	Very light blue
851	−	924	Very dark gray green
274	⊘	928	Very light gray green
86	T	3608	Very light plum
85	C	3609	Ultra light plum
1030	Ø	3746	Dark blue violet
306	∧	3820	Dark straw
98	n	3835	Medium grape

LAZY-DAISY STITCH (3X)

ANCHOR		DMC	COLOR
2	−	White	White*

LAZY-DAISY STITCH (2X)

ANCHOR		DMC	COLORS
215	−	320	Medium pistachio green*
161	−	813	Light blue*

STRAIGHT STITCH (3X)

ANCHOR		DMC	COLOR
216	−	163	Medium celadon green*

BACKSTITCH (2X)

ANCHOR		DMC	COLORS
876	−	163	Medium celadon green* (leaves on white flowers)
215	−	320	Medium pistachio green* (stems)
102	−	550	Very dark violet (purple flowers)
161	−	826	Medium blue (egg)
100	−	3834	Dark grape (bow, lettering)

BACKSTITCH (1X)

ANCHOR		DMC	COLORS
359	−	801	Dark coffee brown (leaves on purple flowers)
167	−	3766	Light peacock blue (white flowers)

FRENCH KNOT (2X)

ANCHOR		DMC	COLORS
215	●	320	Medium pistachio green* (2 wraps)
86	●	3608	Very light plum* (2 wraps)
306	●	3820	Dark straw* (3 wraps)

*Duplicate color

CROSS-STITCH (2X)		
ANCHOR	DMC	COLORS
206 ✳	564	Very light jade
301 ◇	744	Pale yellow
300 ╱	745	Light pale yellow
1022 ◔	760	Salmon
1021 $	761	Light salmon
128 +	775	Very light baby blue
160 ↑	827	Very light blue
73 #	963	Ultra very light dusty rose
928 —	3761	Light sky blue
2 ◯	White	White

BACKSTITCH (1X)		
ANCHOR	DMC	COLOR
382 —	3371	Black brown

BACKSTITCH (2X)		
ANCHOR	DMC	COLOR
382 —	3371	Black brown*

FRENCH KNOT (1X)		
ANCHOR	DMC	COLORS
206 ●	564	Very light jade*
301 ●	744	Pale yellow*
300 ○	745	Light pale yellow*
1022 ●	760	Salmon*
128 ●	775	Very light baby blue*
73 ●	963	Ultra very light dusty rose*
382 ●	3371	Black brown*

FRENCH KNOT (2X)		
ANCHOR	DMC	COLOR
382 ●	3371	Black brown*

*Duplicate color

Spring

Easter Egg

Design by Nancy Taylor

Frame this piece as shown, or use as an insert in the window of a keepsake card.

Materials

- Victorian blue 14-count Aida: 9 x 10 inches
- Needlecraft card with 3 x 5-inch opening

"Spring Easter Egg" was stitched on Victorian blue 14-count Aida by Zweigart using DMC floss.

Skill Level

**Average

Stitch Count

36 wide x 59 high

Approximate Design Size

11-count 3⅜" x 5⅜"
14-count 2⅝" x 4¼"
16-count 2¼" x 3¾"
18-count 2" x 3⅜"
22-count 1⅝" x 2¾"

Instructions

1. Center and stitch design using two strands floss for Cross-Stitch, Backstitch and French Knot on lettering. Use one strand floss for remaining Backstitch and French Knots.

Note: Each French-Knot cluster is made up of six French Knots. ❖

Wildflower Bouquet

Design by Kathleen Hurley

Stitch a lovely tablecloth and add a set of matching napkins and coasters.

Materials

- Tablecloth with white 11-count 10⅝ x 12-inch design area #2447/1
- Napkin with white 11-count 2 x 2⅜-inch design area #1960/1
- White 14-count Aida: 7 x 7 inches
- Acrylic coaster with 3 x 3-inch design opening

"Wildflower Bouquet" projects were stitched on Rondo Tablecloth and Champagne napkin by Zweigart and DMC 14-count Aida using DMC floss.

Skill Level

**Average

Stitch Count

117 wide x 133 high

Approximate Design Size

11-count 10⅝" x 12"
14-count 8⅜" x 9½"
16-count 7" x 8⅜"
18-count 6½" x 7⅜"
22-count 5⅜" x 6"

Instructions

1. For tablecloth, center and stitch design in round area of tablecloth, using three strands floss for Cross-Stitch, two strands for French Knot, Straight Stitch and Backstitch on stems, and one strand floss for remaining Backstitch.

Poppy (B)

Daisy (A)

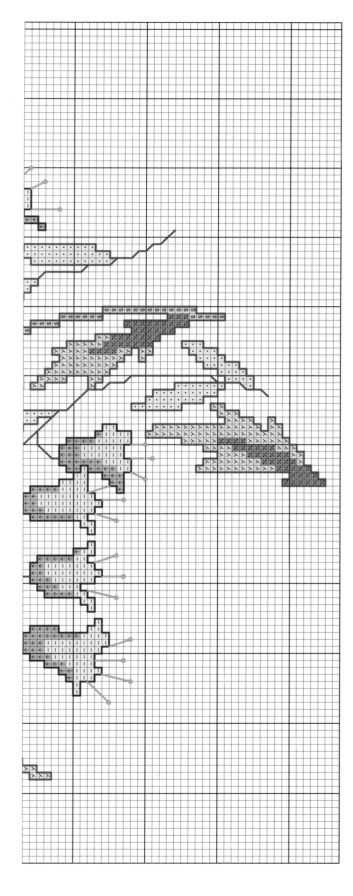

2. For each napkin, center and stitch individual yellow daisy A in round area of napkin, using three strands floss for Cross-Stitch and one strand floss for Backstitch.

3. For coaster, center and stitch large red poppy B on 14-count Aida, using three strands floss for Cross-Stitch and one strand floss for Backstitch.

Finishing

1. Insert stitched Aida into acrylic coaster following manufacturer's instructions. ❖

CROSS-STITCH (3X)

ANCHOR		DMC	COLORS
2	☑	White	White
403	■	310	Black
11	◆◆	350	Medium coral
236	✚	413	Dark pewter gray
398	③	415	Pearl gray
923	$	699	Green
227	✕	701	Light green
238	⊻	703	Chartreuse
305	▨	725	Medium light topaz
293	〘	727	Very light topaz
304	〗	741	Medium tangerine
303	✳	742	Light tangerine
13	✚	817	Very dark coral red
161	↑	826	Medium blue
160	−	827	Very light blue
206	·	966	Medium baby green

BACKSTITCH (1X)

ANCHOR		DMC	COLORS
403	—	310	Black*
148	—	311	Medium navy blue
235	—	414	Dark steel gray
304	=	741	Medium tangerine*
43	—	815	Medium garnet

BACKSTITCH (2X)

ANCHOR		DMC	COLOR
227	—	701	Light green*

STRAIGHT STITCH (2X)

ANCHOR		DMC	COLORS
305	—	725	Medium light topaz*
398	—	415	Pearl gray*

FRENCH KNOT (2X)

ANCHOR		DMC	COLORS
305	●	725	Medium light topaz*
398	●	415	Pearl gray*

*Duplicate color

Topiary Trio

Original artwork by Susan Pisoni, adapted for cross-stitch by Mike Vickery

These unique topiaries can be framed individually or as a group.

Either way, you'll love their fresh look.

Materials

- Ivory 14-count Aida:
  10 x 12 inches

"Topiary Trio" was stitched on 14-count Aida by Wichelt Imports using DMC floss. Finished pieces were custom framed.

Skill Level
**Average

Topiary Bird

Stitch Count
51 wide x 78 high

Approximate Design Size
11-count 4⅝" x 7"
14-count 3⅝" x 5½"
16-count 3⅛" x 4⅞"
18-count 2⅞" x 4⅜"
22-count 2⅜" x 3½"

Topiary Bee

Stitch Count
57 wide x 80 high

Approximate Design Size
11-count 5¼" x 7¼"
14-count 4⅛" x 5¾"
16-count 3⅝" x 5"
18-count 3¼" x 4⅜"
22-count 2⅝" x 3⅝"

Topiary Frog

Stitch Count
58 wide x 80 high

Approximate Design Size
11-count 5¼" x 7¼"
14-count 4⅛" x 5¾"
16-count 3⅝" x 5"
18-count 3¼" x 4⅜"
22-count 2⅝" x 3⅝"

Instructions

1. Center and stitch design using two strands floss for Cross-Stitch and one strand floss for Backstitch. ❖

Topiary Frog

CROSS-STITCH (2X)

ANCHOR		DMC	COLORS
218		319	Very dark pistachio green
215		320	Medium pistachio green
214		368	Light pistachio green
213		369	Very light pistachio green
914		407	Dark desert sand
936		632	Ultra very dark desert sand
1088		838	Very dark beige brown
4146		950	Light desert sand
75		962	Medium dusty rose
73		963	Ultra very light dusty rose
25		3716	Very light dusty rose

BACKSTITCH (1X)

ANCHOR		DMC	COLORS
42		309	Deep rose
936		632	Ultra very dark desert sand*
218		890	Ultra dark pistachio green

*Duplicate color

Topiary Bee

CROSS-STITCH (2X)

ANCHOR		DMC	COLORS
218		319	Very dark pistachio green
215		320	Medium pistachio green
214		368	Light pistachio green
213		369	Very light pistachio green
914		407	Dark desert sand
936		632	Ultra very dark desert sand
298		725	Topaz
293		727	Very light topaz
1088		838	Very dark beige brown
4146		950	Light desert sand

BACKSTITCH (1X)

ANCHOR		DMC	COLORS
936		632	Ultra very dark desert sand*
307		783	Medium topaz
218		890	Ultra dark pistachio green

*Duplicate color

Topiary Bird

CROSS-STITCH (2X)

ANCHOR		DMC	COLORS
218	↑	319	Very dark pistachio green
215	ठ	320	Medium pistachio green
214	2	368	Light pistachio green
1043	/	369	Very light pistachio green
914	⊞	407	Dark desert sand
936	◆	632	Ultra very dark desert sand
302	Y	743	Medium yellow
1088	■	838	Very dark beige brown
4146	%	950	Light desert sand
129	◁	3325	Light baby blue

BACKSTITCH (1X)

ANCHOR		DMC	COLORS
936	—	632	Ultra very dark desert sand*
218	—	890	Ultra dark pistachio green

*Duplicate color

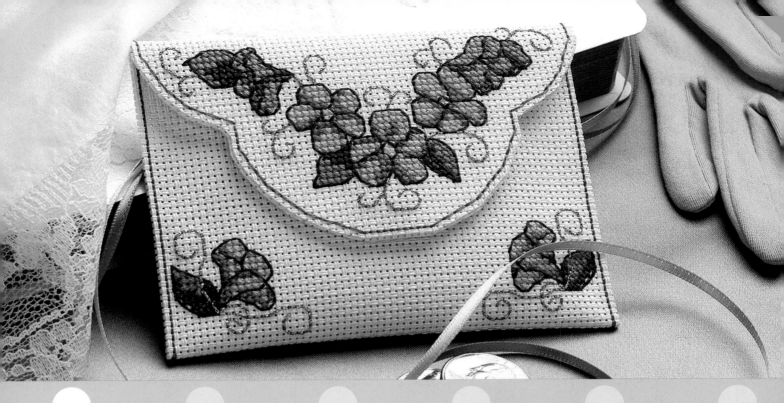

Morning Glory
Mini Purse

Design by Kathy Wirth

Whether you add a twisted cord to make an adorable spring purse for a little girl or carry

this yourself, you'll receive compliments from all who see it!

Materials
- White 14-count Vinyl-Weave:
  6 x 12 inches (for purse)
  3 x 6 inches (for flap)
- Kreinik #8 fine braid: gold #002
- ⅝-inch hook-and-loop tape fastener
- Craft glue or glue gun

"Morning Glory Mini Purse" was stitched on Crafter's Pride Vinyl-Weave by Daniel Enterprises, using DMC floss.

Skill Level
**Average

Stitch Count
68 wide x 134 high

Approximate Design Size:
11-count 6¼" x 12¼"
14-count 4⅞" x 9⅝"
16-count 4¼" x 8½"
18-count 3⅞" x 7½"
22-count 3⅛" x 6⅛"

Instructions
1. Center and stitch design on 6 x 12-inch piece, using three strands floss for Cross-Stitch and two strands floss or one strand fine braid for Backstitch.

Finishing
Note: Follow cutting lines and trim design.

1. Using six strands white floss, Overcast (see illustration on page 56) inside top edge as indicated on graph.

2. Matching Overcast edge with second fold line, fold bottom up to form pocket. Aligning holes, use two strands medium violet floss and Double Running Stitch (see illustration on page 56) to sew side edges together forming purse.

3. Fold flap, then hold 3 x 6-inch piece on wrong side of scalloped edge of purse. Aligning holes, use two strands medium violet floss and Double Running Stitch (see illustration on page 56) to sew pieces together. Trim vinyl-weave to match.

4. Glue one half of fastener to flap; glue remaining half of fastener to purse. ❖

CROSS-STITCH (3X)

ANCHOR		DMC	COLORS
99	#	552	Medium violet
96	∞	554	Light violet
57	T	601	Dark cranberry
55	X	604	Light cranberry
295	a	726	Light topaz
132	2	797	Royal blue
136	7	799	Medium delft blue
246	□	986	Very dark forest green
242	m	989	Forest green

BACKSTITCH (2X)

ANCHOR		DMC	COLORS
236	—	3799	Very dark pewter gray
99	—	552	Medium violet

BACKSTITCH (1X)

KREINIK (#8) FINE BRAID

002	—		Gold

CUTTING LINE ▬
FOLDING LINE (orange dotted line)
DOUBLE RUNNING STITCH (2X)

99	—	552	Medium violet

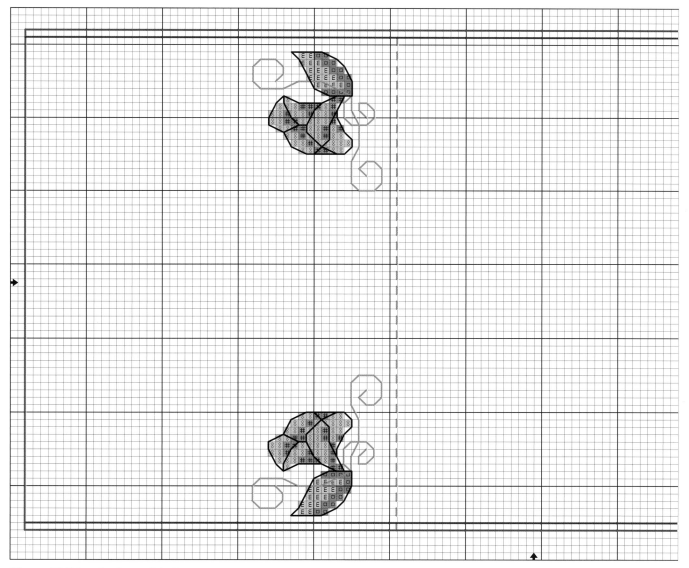

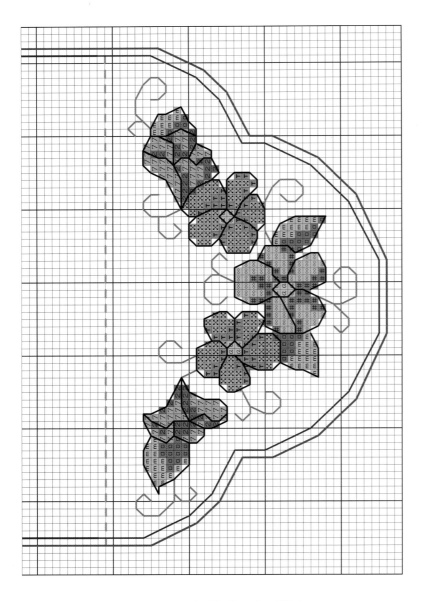

CROSS-STITCH (3X)

ANCHOR		DMC	COLORS
99	#	552	Medium violet
96	∞	554	Light violet
57	T	601	Dark cranberry
55	X	604	Light cranberry
295	a	726	Light topaz
132	2	797	Royal blue
136	7	799	Medium delft blue
246	□	986	Very dark forest green
242	m	989	Forest green

BACKSTITCH (2X)

ANCHOR		DMC	COLORS
236	—	3799	Very dark pewter gray
99	—	552	Medium violet

BACKSTITCH (1X)
KREINIK (#8) FINE BRAID

002	—		Gold

CUTTING LINE —

FOLDING LINE (orange dotted line)

DOUBLE RUNNING STITCH (2X)

99	—	552	Medium violet

Double Running Stitch

1. Work Running Stitch

2. In reverse, work Running Stitch in spaces of step 1.

Overcast

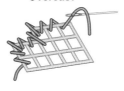

The Hunter and The Yei

Design by Susan Stadler

Brimming with ancient tribal style, these pieces will be right at home in a den or game room.

Materials
- Antique white 14-count Aida:
  10½ x 10½ inches for each
- Kreinik blending filament:
  021 copper and 014 blue

"The Hunter & The Yei" were stitched on 14-count Aida from Wichelt Imports using DMC floss. Finished pieces were custom framed.

Skill Level
**Average

Stitch Count for Each
76 wide x 66 high

Approximate Design Size
11-count 6⅞" x 6"
14-count 5⅜" x 4¾"
16-count 4¾" x 4⅛"
18-count 4¼" x 3⅝"
22-count 3½" x 3"

Instructions
1. Center and stitch design using two strands floss, or two strands floss and one strand blending filament for Cross-Stitch, and two strands floss for Straight Stitch. ❖

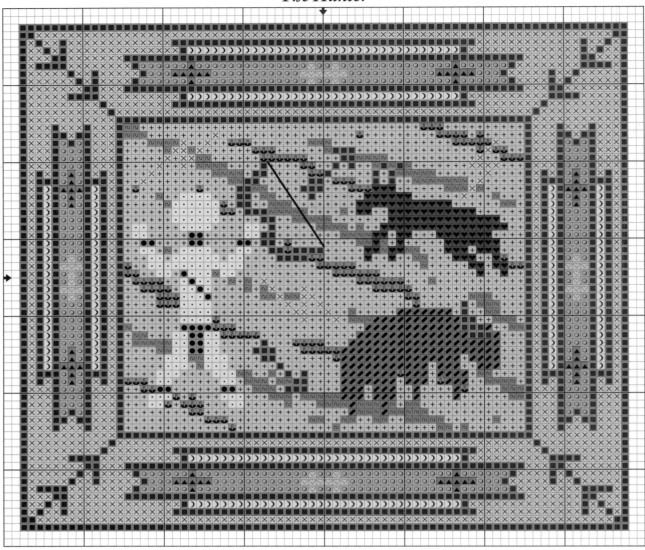

The Hunter

CROSS-STITCH (2X)

ANCHOR		DMC	COLORS
403	■	310	Black
11	▲	350	Medium coral
1064	◐	597	Turquoise
13	♥	817	Very dark coral red
1082	⬇	841	Light beige brown
1002	+	977	Light golden brown
263	◢	3362	Dark pine green
1068	●	3808	Ultra very dark turquoise
295	✕	3822	Light straw
1049	﬌	3826	Golden brown
926	·	3866	Ultra very light mocha brown

KREINIK BLENDED CROSS-STITCH

ANCHOR		DMC	COLORS
9	♡	352	Light coral (2X) with 021 copper BF (1X)
1060	◗	3811	Very light turquoise (2X) with 014 sky blue BF (1X)

STRAIGHT STITCH (2X)

ANCHOR		DMC	COLOR
403	━	310	Black*

*Duplicate color

The Yei

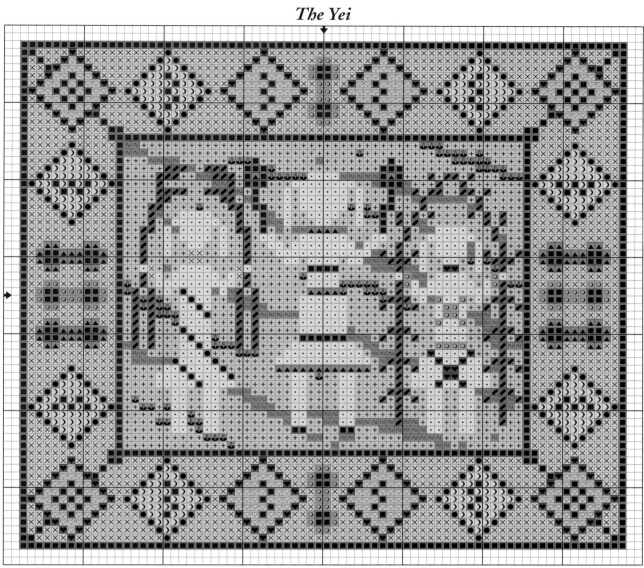

The Yei

CROSS-STITCH (2X)

ANCHOR		DMC	COLORS
403	■	310	Black
11	▲	350	Medium coral
1064	◎	597	Turquoise
13	▼	817	Very dark coral red
1082	⬇	841	Light beige brown
1002	+	977	Light golden brown
263	◪	3362	Dark pine green
1068	●	3808	Ultra very dark turquoise
295	✕	3822	Light straw
1049	∾	3826	Golden brown
926	·	3866	Ultra very light mocha brown

KREINIK BLENDED CROSS-STITCH

ANCHOR		DMC	COLORS
9	♡	352	Light coral (2X) with 021 copper BF (1X)
1060	☽	3811	Very light turquoise (2X) with 014 sky blue BF (1X)

*Duplicate color

Par Four Desk Accessories

Designs by Mike Vickery

Happen to have a dad who loves to golf?

These desk accessories will remind him of time on the links!

Materials

- White 18-count Aida:
  7 x 8 inches
  8 x 8 inches
- 2¾- x 4¼-inch clear acrylic rectangle with 1⅛- x 2¾-inch design opening (for paper clip holder)
- 3½- x 3½-inch clear acrylic square with 2⅜- x 2¼-inch design opening (for coaster)

"Par Four Desk Accessories" were stitched on white 18-count Aida by DMC using DMC floss.

Skill Level

*Easy

Paper Clip Holder
Stitch Count

20 wide x 50 high

Approximate Design Size

11-count 1⅞" x 4⅛"
14-count 1⅜" x 3½"
16-count 1¼" x 3⅛"
18-count 1⅛" x 2¾"
22-count ⅞" x 2¼"

Coaster
Stitch Count

44 wide x 40 high

Approximate Design Size

11-count 4" x 3⅝"

14-count 3⅛" x 2⅞"
16-count 2¾" x 2½"
18-count 2⅜" x 2¼"
22-count 2" x 1⅞"

Instructions

1. Using 7- x 8-inch piece Aida for paper clip holder and 8- x 8-inch piece Aida for coaster, center and stitch designs using two strands floss for Cross-Stitch and one strand floss for Backstitch.

Finishing

1. Insert stitched pieces into acrylic rectangle and square following manufacturer's instructions. ❖

Coaster

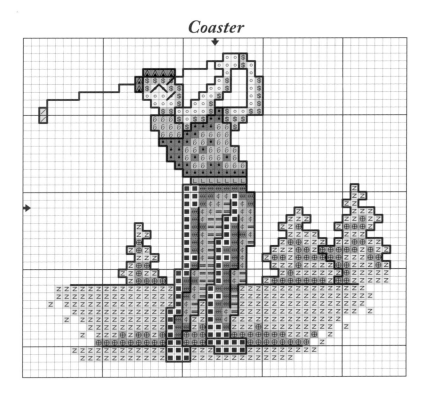

Coaster

CROSS-STITCH (2X)

ANCHOR		DMC	COLORS
403	■	310	Black
399	=	318	Light steel gray
236	⫷	413	Dark pewter gray
235	¢	414	Dark steel gray
310	▲	434	Light brown
1005	◆	498	Dark red
46	6	666	Bright red
226	⊕	702	Kelly green
256	Z	704	Bright chartreuse
361	L	738	Very light tan
234	/	762	Very light pearl gray
881	$	945	Tawny
1009	○	3770	Very light tawny

BACKSTITCH (1X)

ANCHOR		DMC	COLOR
236	—	3799	Very dark pewter gray

Paper Clip Holder

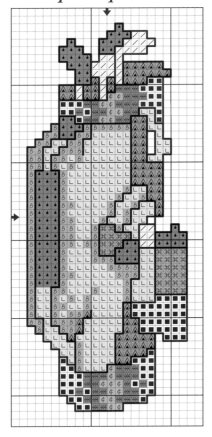

Paper Clip Holder

CROSS-STITCH (2X)

ANCHOR		DMC	COLORS
403	■	310	Black
977	⌘	334	Medium baby blue
236	⫷	413	Dark pewter gray
235	¢	414	Dark steel gray
310	▲	434	Light brown
1045	δ	436	Tan
1005	◆	498	Dark red
361	L	738	Very light tan
234	/	762	Very light pearl gray

BACKSTITCH (1X)

ANCHOR		DMC	COLOR
236	—	3799	Very dark pewter gray

Little Treasure Clock

Design by Elaine Fuller

This symmetrical design looks right at home featured in the face of a tiny clock. For a coordinating pillow, try stitching it on the same fabric over four threads instead of one!

Materials

- Daffodil 22-count Softana: 8½ x 8½ inches
- 3 x 5-inch wooden clock with 2½-inch round design area

"Little Treasure Clock" was stitched on daffodil 22-count Softana by Zweigart using DMC floss. Finished piece is displayed in #48241 Little Treasure Clock from Sudberry House.

Skill Level

**Average

Stitch Count

50 wide x 50 high

Approximate Design Size

11-count 4½" x 4½"
14-count 3½" x 3½"
16-count 3⅛" x 3⅛"
18-count 2¾" x 2¾"
22-count 2¼" x 2¼"

Instructions

1. Center and stitch design on 22-count Softana, stitching over one thread using one strand floss for Cross-Stitch.

Finishing

1. Insert stitched design in clock face, following manufacturer's instructions. ❖

CROSS-STITCH (1X)

ANCHOR		DMC	COLOR
1001	∞	976	Medium golden brown

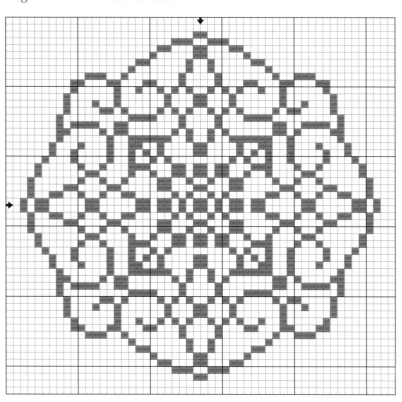

Roosters on Parade

Design by Nancy Taylor

Strutting their patriotic pride, these roosters are right at home with your country decor.

Materials
- Powder blue 22-count linen:
  17 x 25 inches

"Roosters on Parade" was stitched using DMC floss. Finished piece was custom framed.

Skill Level
*Easy

Stitch Count
210 wide x 121 high

Approximate Design Size
11-count 19⅛" x 11"
14-count 15" x 8¾"
16-count 13¼" x 7⅝"
18-count 11¾" x 6¾"
22-count 9⅝" x 5½"
22-count over two threads 19⅛" x 11"

Instructions
1. Center and stitch design, stitching over two threads and using four strands floss for Cross-Stitch and two strands floss for Backstitch. ❖

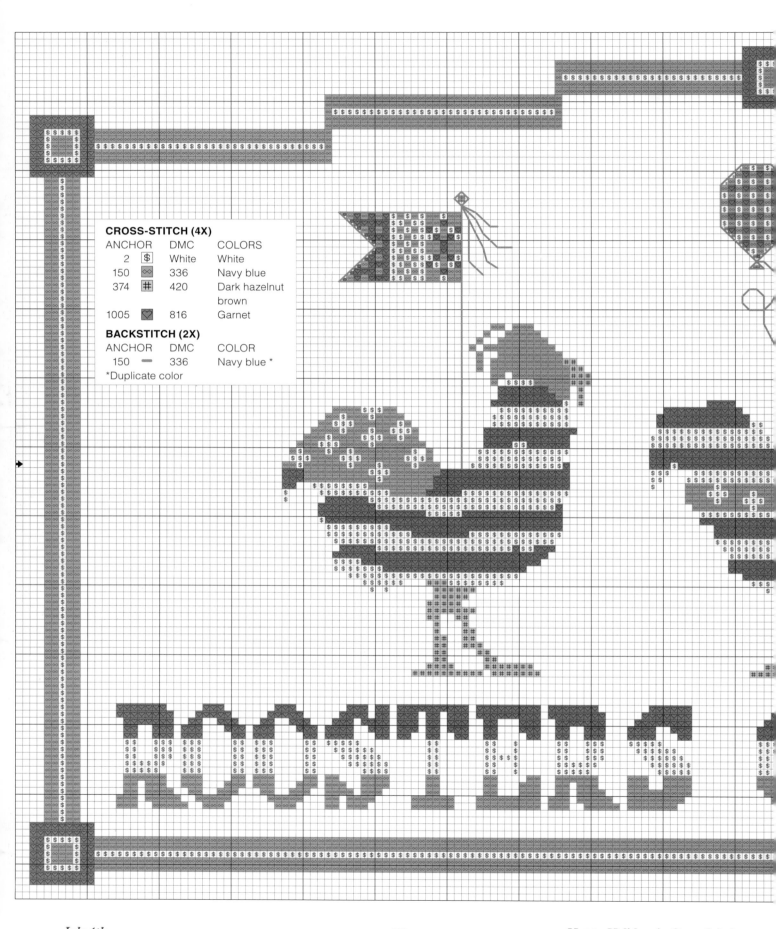

CROSS-STITCH (4X)

ANCHOR		DMC	COLORS
2	$	White	White
150	∞	336	Navy blue
374	#	420	Dark hazelnut brown
1005	♡	816	Garnet

BACKSTITCH (2X)

ANCHOR		DMC	COLOR
150	—	336	Navy blue *

*Duplicate color

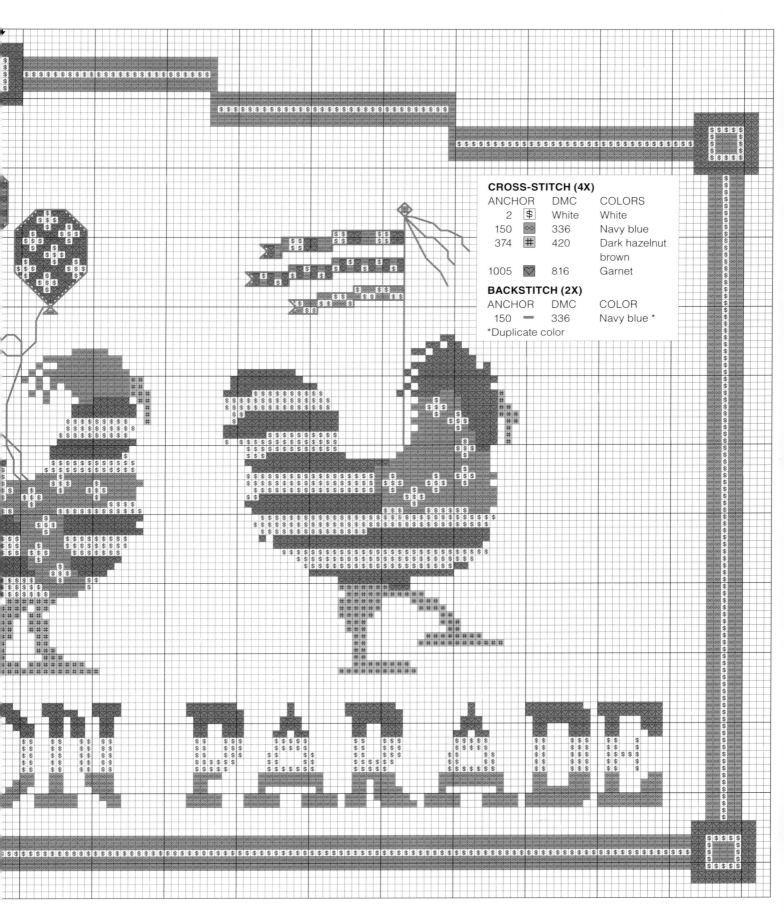

CROSS-STITCH (4X)

ANCHOR		DMC	COLORS
2	$	White	White
150	⊗	336	Navy blue
374	#	420	Dark hazelnut brown
1005	♡	816	Garnet

BACKSTITCH (2X)

ANCHOR		DMC	COLOR
150	—	336	Navy blue *

*Duplicate color

Hurrah!

Design by Gail Bussi

Stitch away those lazy hazy days of summer with Hurrah for the red, white and blue.

Materials
- Antique white 28-count Cashel linen: 10 x 13 inches

"Hurrah!" was stitched on antique white 28-countCaschel linen by Zweigart using DMC floss. Finished piece was custom framed.

Skill Level
**Average

Stitch Count:
93 wide x 53 high

Approximate Design Size
11-count 8½" x 4⅞"
14-count 6¾" x 3⅞"
16-count 5⅞" x 3⅜"
18-count 5¼" x 3"
22-count 4¼" x 2½"
28-count over two threads 6¾" x 3⅞"

Instructions
1. Center and stitch design, stitching over two threads and using two strands floss for Cross-Stitch and one strand floss for Backstitch and French Knot. ❖

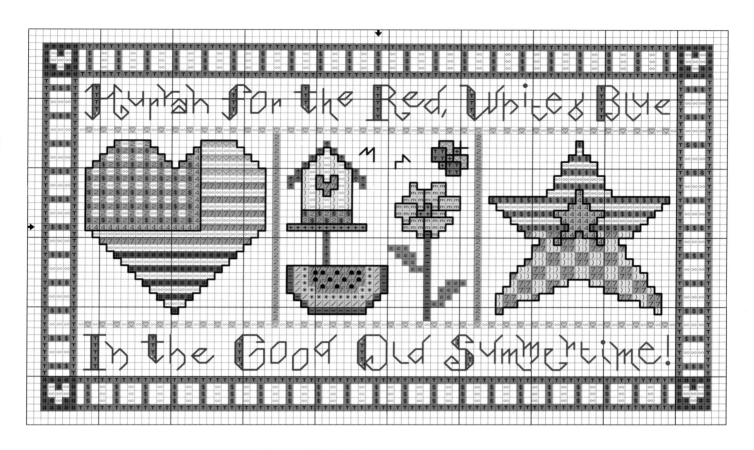

CROSS-STITCH (2X)

ANCHOR		DMC	COLORS
2	∞	White	White
215	▬	320	Medium pistachio green
214	e	368	Light pistachio green
1043	/	369	Very light pistachio green
889	↑	610	Light drab brown
832	+	612	Very light drab brown
305	4	725	Topaz
301	m	744	Pale yellow
1022	7	760	Salmon
1021	♡	761	Light salmon
23	)	818	Baby pink
1033	T	932	Light antique blue
1023	#	3328	Dark salmon
1020	✳	3713	Very light salmon
1032	2	3752	Very light antique blue
1034	$	3755	Medium antique blue

BACKSTITCH (1X)

ANCHOR		DMC	COLORS
1035	▬	930	Dark antique blue
273	▬	3787	Dark brown gray

FRENCH KNOT (1X)

ANCHOR		DMC	COLORS
1035	●	930	Dark antique blue*
273	●	3787	Dark brown gray*

*Duplicate color"

 # *Only When It's Dark*

Design by Jackie Harris

For added flair, combine glow-in-the-dark blending filament with the floss,

and let the sentiment of this piece accompany you into dreamland.

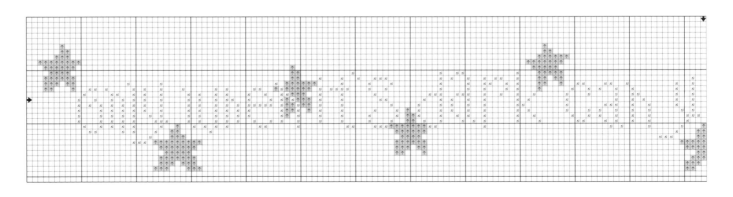

Materials

- Navy blue 14-count Aida:
  25 x 10 inches

"Only When It's Dark" was stitched on navy blue 14-count Aida from Zweigart using Anchor floss. Finished piece was custom framed.

Skill Level

*Easy

Stitch Count

243 wide x 27 high

Approximate Design Size

11-count 22" x 2½"
14-count 17⅜" x 2"
16-count 15⅛" x 1⅝"
18-count 13½" x 1½"
22-count 11" x 1¼"

Instructions

1. Center and stitch design, using three strands floss for Cross-Stitch. ❖

CROSS-STITCH (3X)

DMC		ANCHOR	COLORS
White	◢	2	White
444	↑	297	Dark lemon

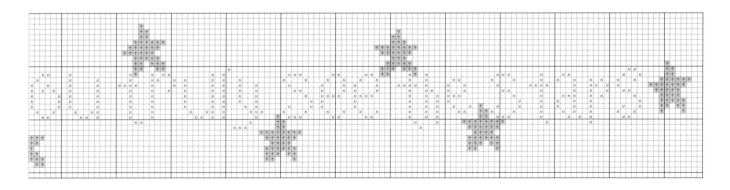

God Bless America

Design by Ursula Michael

Simple stitching will command a stately presence in your home. While strikingly framed as shown, this piece would also look great under glass in a serving tray!

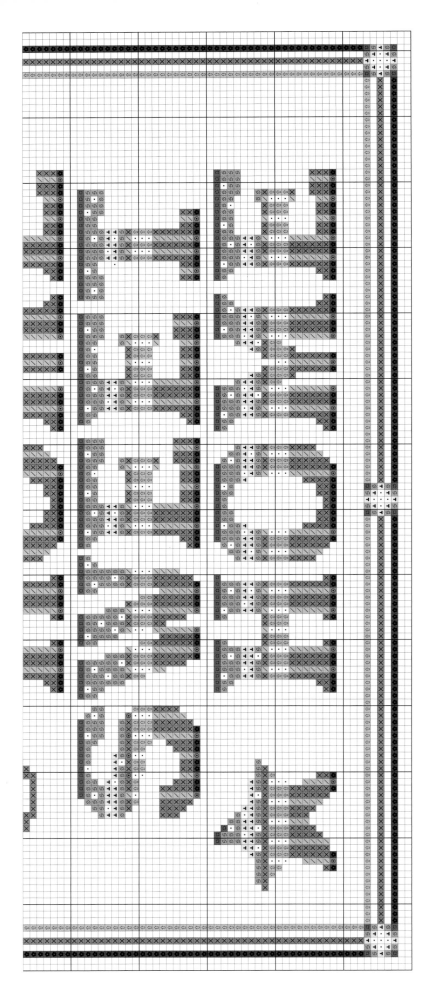

Materials

- White 14-count Aida:
  18 x 19 inches

"God Bless America" was stitched on white 14-count Aida by Zweigart using DMC floss. Finished piece was custom framed.

Skill Level

*Easy

Stitch Count

139 wide x 156 high

Approximate Design Size

11-count 12⅝" x 14⅛"
14-count 9⅞" x 11⅛"
16-count 8⅝" x 9¾"
18-count 7¾" x 8⅝"
22-count 6⅜" x 7"

Instructions

1. Center and stitch design, using three strands floss for Cross-Stitch. ❖

CROSS-STITCH (3X)

ANCHOR		DMC	COLORS
2	·	White	White
1006	✕	304	Medium red
148	▫	311	Medium navy blue
978	⑤	322	Dark baby blue
11	⇧	350	Medium coral
900	◉	648	Light beaver gray
305	✿	725	Medium light topaz
1005	⬟	816	Garnet
847	╱	3072	Very light beaver gray
140	⬒	3755	Baby blue

Birthday Bears

Designs by Pamela Kellogg for Kreinik

Whether you stitch one, two or all twelve, this group of bears will add a sparkle to your eye and

a smile to your stitching!

Clockwise from the top: April Bear, March Bear, January Bear and February Bear.

Skill Level
**Average

Stitch Count
47 wide x 73 high (for each bear, including head)

Approximate Design Size
(for each bear, including head)
11-count 4¼" x 6⅝"
14-count 3⅜" x 5¼"
16-count 3" x 4½"
18-count 2⅝" x 4"
22-count 2⅛" x 3⅜"
28-count over two threads 3⅜" x 5¼"

January Bear
Materials
- Barely blue 28-count Jobelan: 9 x 11 inches
- Kreinik #4 very fine braid: pearl #032, star blue #094, platinum #101, blue ice #1432 and black #005
- Blue moiré-covered oval chipboard box with 4 x 5⅞-inch design area

"January Bear" was stitched on barely blue 28-count Jobelan by Wichelt using DMC floss. Finished piece was inserted in small blue moiré box #99762 from Sudberry House.

Instructions
1. Center and stitch design on 28-count Jobelan, stitching over two threads using three strands floss or one strand very fine braid for Cross-Stitch, and one strand floss or very fine braid for Backstitch. Use three strands floss for French Knot, wrapping needle twice.

Finishing
1. Insert finished piece in box opening, following manufacturer's instructions.

February Bear

Materials
- Black Crafter's Pride address book with white 14-count vinyl-weave insert
- Kreinik #4 very fine braid: gold #002, black #005, star pink #092, star blue #094, pale pink #192, blue ice #1432, and star green #9194

"February Bear" was stitched on 14-count vinyl-weave insert using DMC floss. Finished piece was inserted in Crafter's Pride #30710 black address book from Daniel Enterprises.

Instructions
1. Center and stitch design on 14-count vinyl-weave, using three strands floss or one strand very fine braid for Cross-Stitch and one strand floss or very fine braid for Backstitch. Use three strands floss for French Knot, wrapping needle twice.

Finishing
1. Insert finished piece in address book opening, following manufacturer's instructions.

March Bear

Materials
- White Crafter's Pride 14-count tissue box cover
- Kreinik #4 very fine braid: gold #002, green #008, chartreuse #015, star green #9194 and star blue #094

"March Bear" was stitched on white Crafter's Pride 14-count tissue box cover #20900 from Daniel Enterprises using DMC floss.

Instructions
1. Center and stitch design on 14-count tissue box cover, using three strands floss or one strand very fine braid for Cross-Stitch, two strands floss and one strand very fine braid for Blended Cross-Stitch, and one strand floss or very fine braid for Backstitch. Use three strands floss for French Knot, wrapping needle twice.

April Bear

Materials
- Buttermilk 28-count Jobelan: 9 x 11 inches
- Kreinik #4 very fine braid: purple #012, chartreuse #015, citron #028, star mauve #093, pale yellow #191, peridot #3215 and topaz #3228

"April Bear" was stitched on buttermilk 28-count Jobelan by Wichelt using DMC floss. Finished piece was custom framed.

Instructions
1. Center and stitch design on 28-count Jobelan, stitching over two threads using three strands floss or one strand very fine braid for Cross-Stitch, and one strand floss or very fine braid for Backstitch. Use three strands floss for French Knot, wrapping needle twice. ❖

Bear Head

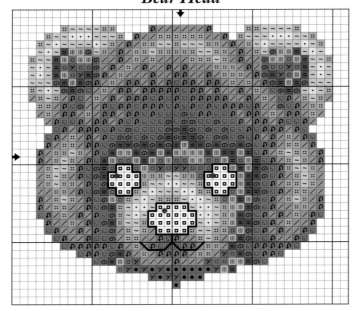

Bear Head

CROSS-STITCH (3X)

ANCHOR		DMC	COLORS
358		433	Medium brown
310		434	Light brown
1046		435	Very light brown
1045		436	Tan
362		437	Light tan
926		712	Cream
361		738	Very light tan
359	~	801	Dark coffee brown
360	III	898	Very dark coffee brown
381		938	Ultra dark coffee brown
382		3371	Black brown

CROSS-STITCH (1X)

KREINIK #4 BRAID		COLOR
005		Black

BACKSTITCH (1X)

ANCHOR		DMC	COLOR
382	—	3371	Black brown*
KREINIK #4 BRAID			COLOR
005	—		Black*

FRENCH KNOT (3X)

ANCHOR		DMC	COLOR
2	●	White	White (eyes and nose)

*Duplicate color

January Bear

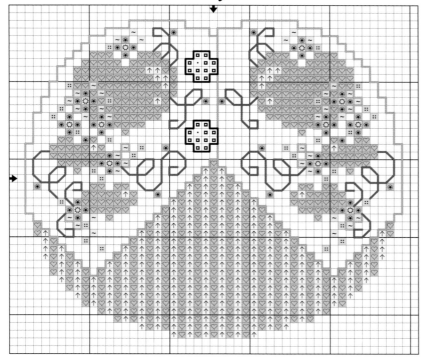

January Bear

CROSS-STITCH (3X)

ANCHOR		DMC	COLORS
2	·	White	White
358	=	433	Medium brown
683	▣	500	Very dark blue green
878	−	501	Dark blue green
877	◕	502	Blue green
876	+	503	Medium blue green
1042	☆	504	Light blue green
359	Ⅲ	801	Dark coffee brown
360	▦	898	Very dark coffee brown
875	○	3813	Light blue green

CROSS-STITCH (1X)

KREINIK #4 BRAID		COLORS
032	◊	Pearl
094	✕	Star blue
101	∧	Platinum
1432	▢	Blue ice

BACKSTITCH (1X)

ANCHOR		DMC	COLOR
683	—	500	Very dark blue green* (vines)

KREINIK #4 BRAID		COLORS
094	—	Star blue* (vest, snowflakes, berries)
101	—	Platinum* (buttons)

*Duplicate color

February Bear

February Bear

CROSS-STITCH (3X)

ANCHOR		DMC	COLOR
2	·	White	White

CROSS-STITCH (1X)

KREINIK #4 BRAID		COLORS
002	✿	Gold
005	▪	Black
092	♡	Star pink
094	✺	Star blue
192	↑	Pale pink
1432	~	Blue ice
9194	∷	Star green

BACKSTITCH (1X)

KREINIK #4 BRAID		COLORS
002	—	Gold* (vest)
005	—	Black* (buttons)
094	—	Star blue* (flowers)
9194	—	Star green* (vines)

*Duplicate color

March Bear

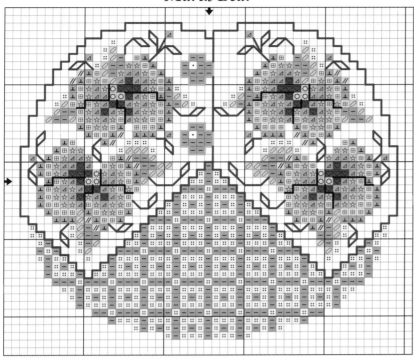

March Bear

CROSS-STITCH (3X)

ANCHOR		DMC	COLOR
2	·	White	White

CROSS-STITCH (1X)

KREINIK #4 BRAID		COLORS
002	✿	Gold
008	−	Green
015	⬭	Chartreuse
9194	::	Star green

KREINIK BLENDED CROSS-STITCH

ANCHOR		DMC	COLORS
118	◿	340	Medium blue violet (2X) with 094 star blue #4 braid (1X)
117	☆	341	Light blue violet (2X) with 094 star blue* #4 braid (1X)
128	⊥	775	Very light baby blue (2X) with 094 star blue* #4 braid (1X)
1037	▧	3756	Ultra very light baby blue (2X) with 094 star blue* #4 braid (1X)
1020	⊞	3747	Very light blue violet (2X) with 094 star blue* #4 braid (1X)
1037	⫽	3756	Ultra very light baby blue (2X) with 094 star blue* #4 braid (1X)

BACKSTITCH (1X)

ANCHOR	DMC	COLOR
119	333	Very dark blue violet (violets)

KREINIK #4 BRAID		COLORS
002	=	Gold* (buttons)
008	−	Green* (vest, small leaves)

*Duplicate color

April Bear

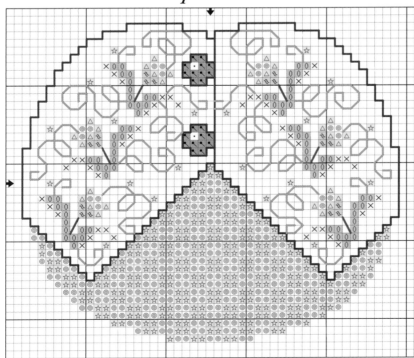

April Bear

CROSS-STITCH (3X)

ANCHOR		DMC	COLOR
2	·	White	White

CROSS-STITCH (1X)

KREINIK #4 BRAID		COLORS
012	◣	Purple
015	0	Chartreuse
028	⤵	Citron
093	☆	Star mauve
191	◎	Pale yellow
3215	✕	Peridot
3228	△	Topaz

BACKSTITCH (1X)

KREINIK #4 BRAID		COLORS
012	−	Purple* (vest, buttons)
015	−	Chartreuse* (stems)
3215	−	Peridot* (vines)

*Duplicate color

Clockwise from the left:
August Bear, June Bear,
July Bear and May Bear.

May Bear
Materials

- 10 x 10-inch antique white pillow sham with 6 x 6-inch 14-count Aida stitching area
- Kreinik #4 very fine braid: black #005, sky blue hi lustre #014HL, chartreuse #015, blue zircon #3214, peridot #3215 and star pink #092
- 10 x 10-inch pillow form

"May Bear" was stitched on 14-count Aida antique white Lady Elizabeth Pillow Sham by Charles Craft #PS-7780-0322 using DMC floss.

Instructions

1. Center and stitch design, using three strands floss or one strand very fine braid for Cross-Stitch, two strands floss and one strand very fine braid for Blended Cross-Stitch, and one strand floss or one strand very fine braid for Backstitch. Use three strands floss for French Knot, wrapping needle twice.

June Bear
Materials

- Honey suckle pink 28-count Jobelan: 8 x 12 inches
- Kreinik #4 very fine braid: black #005, green #008, chartreuse #015, fuchsia #024, fuchsia hi lustre #024HL and star pink #092
- 8 x 12-inch piece of backing fabric
- 6¾ x 9¾-inch piece batting
- Sewing needle and thread to match backing fabric
- 7½-inch-wide teddy bear fabric holder

"June Bear" was stitched on honey suckle-pink 28-count Jobelan by Wichelt using DMC floss and Ackfeld 7½-inch Teddy Bear Fabric Holder #67317.

Instructions

1. Center and stitch design on 28-count Jobelan, stitching over two threads using three strands floss or one strand very fine braid for Cross-Stitch, and one strand floss or very fine braid for Backstitch. Use three strands floss for French Knot, wrapping needle twice.

Finishing

1. Fold side and bottom edges of stitched piece to back of work so that piece measures the same along these measurements as batting; press in place. Open folded edges and lay batting on wrong side of work; refold pressed edges, encasing batting. Roll top raw edge to back and baste in place, leaving enough space to insert rod of hanger.

2. Fold edges of backing fabric to wrong side of work so that piece measures the same as folded and pressed stitched piece; press edges in place. Pin backing fabric to back of stitched piece, sandwiching batting between. Invisibly sew backing fabric to back of stitched piece. Remove basting.

3. Insert rod of hanger through casing formed in Step 1; reassemble hanger and hang as desired.

July Bear
Materials

- White 14-count huck towel
- Kreinik #4 very fine braid: red #003, vintage red #003V, green #008, chartreuse #015, pearl #032, royal blue #033 and peridot #3215

"July Bear" was stitched on white 14-count Showcase Huck Towel #HF-6500-6750-EA by Charles Craft using DMC floss.

Instructions

1. Center and stitch design on 14-count panel, using three strands floss or one strand very fine braid for Cross-Stitch, and one strand floss or one strand very fine braid for Backstitch. Use three strands floss for French Knot, wrapping needle twice.

August Bear
Materials

- Cameo peach 28-count Jobelan: 9 x 11 inches
- Kreinik #4 very fine braid: red #003, green #008, chartreuse #015, brown #022, citron #028, pale yellow #191, curry #2122, peridot #3215 and topaz #3228

"August Bear" was stitched on cameo peach 28-count Jobelan by Wichelt using DMC floss. Finished piece was custom framed.

Instructions

1. Center and stitch design on 28-count Jobelan, stitching over two threads using three strands floss or one strand very fine braid for Cross-Stitch, and one strand floss or one strand very fine braid for Backstitch. Use three strands floss for French Knot, wrapping needle twice. ❖

Bear Head

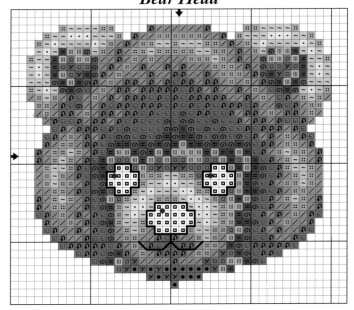

Bear Head

CROSS-STITCH (3X)

ANCHOR		DMC	COLORS
358	▤	433	Medium brown
310	៱	434	Light brown
1046	▣	435	Very light brown
1045	⋂	436	Tan
362	╱	437	Light tan
926	·	712	Cream
361	∷	738	Very light tan
359	~	801	Dark coffee brown
360	⦀	898	Very dark coffee brown
381	▢	938	Ultra dark coffee brown
382	⅄	3371	Black brown

CROSS-STITCH (1X)

KREINIK #4 BRAID		COLOR
005	▫	Black

BACKSTITCH (1X)

ANCHOR		DMC	COLOR
382	▬	3371	Black brown*
KREINIK #4 BRAID			COLOR
005	▬		Black*

FRENCH KNOT (3X)

ANCHOR		DMC	COLOR
2	●	White	White (eyes and nose)

*Duplicate color

May Bear

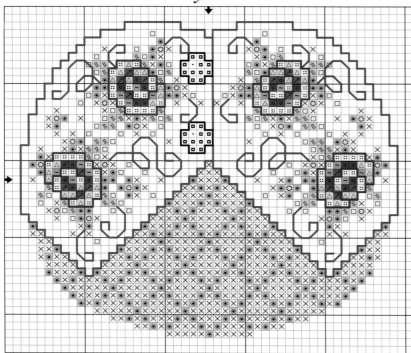

May Bear

CROSS-STITCH (3X)

ANCHOR	DMC	COLORS
2	· White	White
301	✿ 744	Pale yellow

CROSS-STITCH (1X)

KREINIK #4 BRAID		COLORS
005	▫	Black
014HL	✳	Sky blue hi lustre
015	∿	Chartreuse
3214	✕	Blue zircon
3215	▢	Peridot

KREINIK BLENDED CROSS-STITCH

ANCHOR	DMC	COLORS
1028	🔑 3685	Very dark mauve (2X) with 092 star pink #4 braid (1X)
68	~ 3687	Mauve (2X) with 092 star pink #4 braid (1X)
66	△ 3688	Medium mauve (2X) with 092 star pink #4 braid (1X)
49	∷ 3689	Light mauve (2X) with 092 star pink #4 braid (1X)
972	◼ 3803	Dark mauve (2X) with 092 star pink #4 braid (1X)

BACKSTITCH (1X)

ANCHOR	DMC	COLOR
1028	━ 3685	Very dark mauve* (flowers)

KREINIK #4 BRAID		COLORS
005	━	Black* (buttons)
015	━	Chartreuse* (vines and vest)

*Duplicate color

June Bear

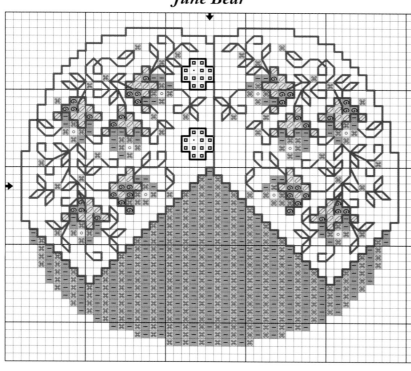

June Bear

CROSS-STITCH (3X)

ANCHOR	DMC	COLOR
2	· White	White

CROSS-STITCH (1X)

KREINIK #4 BRAID		COLORS
005	▫	Black
008	ଗ	Green
015	⊘	Chartreuse
024	⌘	Fuchsia
024HL	—	Fuchsia hi lustre
092	○	Star pink

BACKSTITCH (1X)

KREINIK #4 BRAID		COLORS
005	━	Black (buttons)
008	━	Green* (vines)
024HL	━	Fuchsia hi lustre* (vest)

*Duplicate color

July Bear

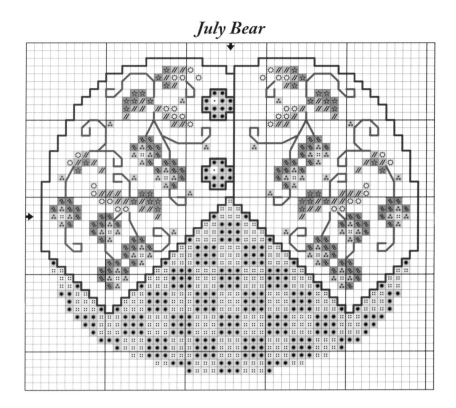

July Bear

CROSS-STITCH (3X)

ANCHOR		DMC	COLOR
2	·	White	White

CROSS-STITCH (1X)

KREINIK #4 BRAID		COLORS
003	✳	Red
003V	↘	Vintage red
008	☆	Green
015	∥	Chartreuse
032	∷	Pearl
033	✴	Royal blue
3215	✿	Peridot

BACKSTITCH (1X)

KREINIK #4 BRAID		COLORS
008	—	Green* (vines)
033	—	Royal blue* (buttons and vest)

*Duplicate color

August Bear

August Bear

CROSS-STITCH (3X)

ANCHOR		DMC	COLOR
2	·	White	White

CROSS-STITCH (1X)

KREINIK #4 BRAID		COLORS
003	●	Red
008	✤	Green
015	~	Chartreuse
022	✎	Brown
028	□	Citron
191	◉	Pale yellow
2122	△	Curry
3215	∷	Peridot
3228	✿	Topaz

BACKSTITCH (1X)

ANCHOR		DMC	COLOR
359	—	801	Dark coffee brown (sunflowers)

KREINIK #4 BRAID		COLORS
008	—	Green* (vines)
022	—	Brown* (buttons and vest)

*Duplicate color

Clockwise from the top: December Bear, October Bear, November Bear and September Bear.

French Knot, wrapping needle twice.

2. Stitch bear ½ inch from lower left-hand corner of place mat.

3. Stitch apple motifs ½ inch from each of the three corners of place mat.

October Bear
Materials

- Water lily 28-count Jobelan: 11 x 13 inches
- Kreinik #4 very fine braid: vintage gold #002V, peacock #085, vintage amber #150V, vintage sienna #152V, vintage verdigris #154V and forest green #5982

"October Bear" was stitched on water lily 28-count Jobelan by Wichelt using DMC floss. Finished piece was custom framed.

Instructions

1. Center and stitch design on 28-count Jobelan, stitching over two threads using three strands floss or one strand very fine braid for Cross-Stitch, and one strand floss or one strand very fine braid for Backstitch. Use three strands floss for French Knot, wrapping needle twice.

November Bear
Materials

- Trivet: 6¾ x 6¾ inches with 18-count Vinyl Weave
- Kreinik #4 very fine braid: vintage red #003V, brown #022, peacock #085, vintage amber #150V, vintage sienna #152V and forest green #5982

"November Bear" was stitched on 18-inch Vinyl Weave included in Crafter's Pride Trivet TR01 by Daniel Enterprises using DMC floss.

Instructions

1. Center and stitch design on 18-count Vinyl Weave, using two strands floss or one strand very fine braid for Cross-Stitch, and one strand floss or one strand very fine braid for

September Bear
Materials

- 14-count Aida place mat: 18 x 13 inches
- Kreinik #4 very fine braid: red #003, vintage red #003V, black #005, green #008, chartreuse #015, pearl #032 and peridot #3215

"September Bear" was stitched on 14-count Aida white place mat by Charles Craft #RC-4851-6750-PK using DMC floss.

Instructions

1. Stitch design, using three strands floss or one strand very fine braid for Cross-Stitch and one strand floss or one strand very fine braid for Backstitch. Use three strands floss for

Backstitch. Use three strands floss for French Knot, wrapping needle twice.

December Bear
Materials
- Delicate Teal 28-count Jobelan: 11 x 13 inches
- Kreinik #4 very fine braid: gold #002, brown #022, fuchsia #024,

fuchsia hi lustre #024HL, peacock #085 and forest green #5982

"December Bear" was stitched on delicate teal 28-count Jobelan by Wichelt using DMC floss. Finished piece was inserted in #2209G Narrow Gold Mirror by Sudberry House.

Instructions
1. Center and stitch design on 28-count Jobelan, stitching over two threads using three strands floss or one strand very fine braid for Cross-Stitch,

and one strand floss or one strand very fine braid for Backstitch. Use three strands floss for French Knot, wrapping needle twice.

Finishing
1. Insert finished piece in frame opening, following manufacturer's instructions. ❖

Bear Head

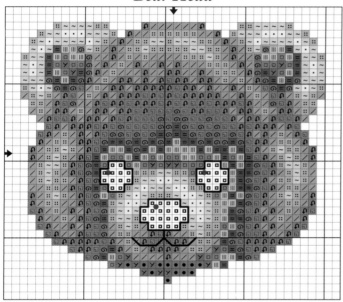

Bear Head

CROSS-STITCH (3X)

ANCHOR		DMC	COLORS
358	▤	433	Medium brown
310	◉	434	Light brown
1046	◐	435	Very light brown
1045	∩	436	Tan
362	╱	437	Light tan
926	·	712	Cream
361	∷	738	Very light tan
359	~	801	Dark coffee brown
360	▥	898	Very dark coffee brown
381	▢	938	Ultra dark coffee brown
382	Y	3371	Black brown

CROSS-STITCH (1X)

KREINIK #4 BRAID		COLOR
005	▣	Black

BACKSTITCH (1X)

ANCHOR		DMC	COLOR
382	▬	3371	Black brown*
KREINIK #4 BRAID			COLOR
005	▬		Black*

FRENCH KNOT (3X)

ANCHOR		DMC	COLOR
2	●	White	White (eyes and nose)

*Duplicate color

September Bear

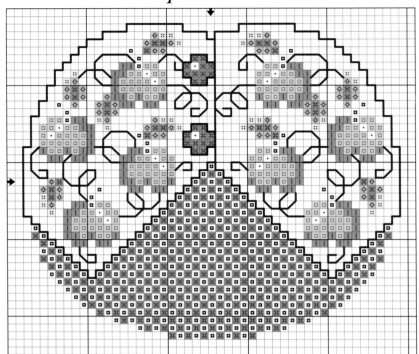

September Bear

CROSS-STITCH (1X)

KREINIK #4 BRAID		COLORS
003	□	Red
003V	❙	Vintage red
005	▣	Black
008	⌘	Green
015	✢	Chartreuse
032	·	Pearl
3215	∷	Peridot

BACKSTITCH (1X)

KREINIK #4 BRAID		COLOR
008	—	Green*

*Duplicate color

October Bear

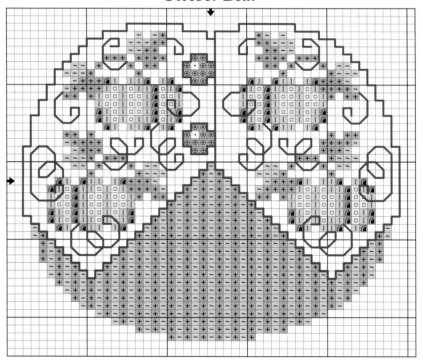

October Bear

CROSS-STITCH (3X)

ANCHOR	DMC	COLOR	COLOR
2	· White	White	

CROSS-STITCH (1X)

KREINIK #4 BRAID		COLORS
002V	□	Vintage gold
085	~	Peacock
150V	❙	Vintage amber
152V	◗	Vintage sienna
154V	⊙	Vintage verdigris
5982	+	Forest green

BACKSTITCH (1X)

KREINIK #4 BRAID		COLOR
154V	—	Vintage verdigris*

*Duplicate color

November Bear

November Bear

CROSS-STITCH (2X)

ANCHOR	DMC	COLOR
2	⊡ White	White

CROSS-STITCH (1X)

KREINIK #4 BRAID		COLORS
003V	–	Vintage red
022	⊙	Brown
085	☆	Peacock
150V	○	Vintage amber
152V	∥	Vintage sienna
5982	✿	Forest green

BACKSTITCH (1X)

KREINIK #4 BRAID		COLORS
022	—	Brown* (buttons, vest and vines)
026V	—	Vintage amethyst (grapes)

*Duplicate color

December Bear

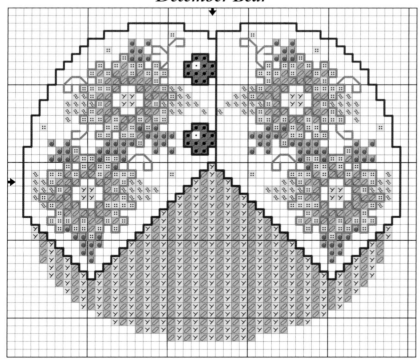

December Bear

CROSS-STITCH (3X)

ANCHOR	DMC	COLOR
2	⊡ White	White

CROSS-STITCH (1X)

KREINIK #4 BRAID		COLORS
002	⅄	Gold
022	◤	Brown
024	⠿	Fuchsia
024HL	⁄	Fuchsia hi lustre
085	⇘	Peacock
5982	◉	Forest green

BACKSTITCH (1X)

KREINIK #4 BRAID		COLORS
002	—	Gold* (flowers and vines)
022	—	Brown* (buttons and vest)

*Duplicate color

 # *Halloween Hangers*

Designs by Patricia Maloney Martin

Add a touch of the holiday to your décor with these Halloween motifs.

Materials

- Black 14-count Aida: 8 x 8 inches for "Happy Halloween" or 10 x 11 inches for "Trick or Treat"
- Craft glue or glue gun

"Halloween Hangers" projects were stitched on 14-count Black Aida by Zweigart using DMC floss.

Skill Level

**Average

Happy Halloween
Stitch Count

35 wide x 28 high

Approximate Design Size

11-count 3¼" x 2⅝"
14-count 2½" x 2"
16-count 2¼" x 1¾"
18-count 2" x 1⅝"
22-count 1⅝" x 1¾"

Instructions

1. Center and stitch design using two strands floss for Cross-Stitch. Use one strand floss for French Knot and Backstitching on pumpkin. Use two strands floss for remaining Backstitch.

Finishing

1. Trim design seven squares from stitching along each edge.

2. Fold two squares at top to back of design and glue in place. Fray remaining edges.

3. For hanger, cut one 8-inch piece of desired color floss. Secure each end through top edge; glue ends to back.

Trick or Treat
Stitch Count

62 wide x 52 high

Approximate Design Size

11-count 5⅝" x 4¾"
14-count 4½" x 3¾"
16-count 3⅞" x 3¼"
18-count 3½" x 3"
22-count 2⅞" x 2⅜"

Instructions

1. Center and stitch design using two strands floss for Cross-Stitch. Use one strand floss for Backstitching on pumpkin and leaves and two strands floss for remaining Backstitch.

Finishing

1. Trim design 15 squares from stitching along top and bottom edges and eight squares from stitching along each side edge.

2. Fold eight squares at top to back of design and glue in place. Fray remaining edges.

3. For hanger, cut one 8-inch piece of desired color floss. Secure each end through top edge; glue ends to back. ❖

Happy Halloween

Happy Halloween

CROSS-STITCH (2X)

ANCHOR		DMC	COLORS
228	◆◆	700	Bright green
256	⌗	704	Bright chartreuse
295	$	726	Light topaz
316	♡	740	Tangerine
330	+	947	Burnt orange

BACKSTITCH (2X)

ANCHOR		DMC	COLORS
228	—	700	Bright green*
330	—	947	Burnt orange*

BACKSTITCH (1X)

ANCHOR		DMC	COLOR
403	—	310	Black

FRENCH KNOT (1X)

ANCHOR		DMC	COLOR
316	●	740	Tangerine*

*Duplicate color

Trick or Treat

Trick or Treat

CROSS-STITCH (2X)

ANCHOR		DMC	COLORS
1046	⊠	435	Very light brown
228	◆◆	700	Bright green
256	#	704	Bright chartreuse
295	$	726	Light topaz
316	♡	740	Tangerine
330	✚	947	Burnt orange

BACKSTITCH (2X)

ANCHOR		DMC	COLORS
228	—	700	Bright green*
316	—	740	Tangerine*
330	—	947	Burnt orange*

BACKSTITCH (1X)

ANCHOR		DMC	COLOR
403	—	310	Black

*Duplicate color

Happy Hauntings!

Design by Gail Bussi

Stitch a little lighthearted fright with this set of ghost and goblin projects!

Materials

- Café mocha 32-count country French linen (for framed piece): 14 x 13 inches
- Kreinik blending filament: black #005, star yellow #091 and white #100
- Black 14-count plastic canvas (for card and magnet)
- 10- x 7-inch piece of blue card stock
- 3- x 4½-inch piece yellow corrugated paper
- 2¼- x 4-inch piece purple card stock
- White alphabet stickers
- Scraps green and black felt (for magnet)
- Magnet strips (for magnet)
- Double-stick adhesive sheet
- Fabric glue

"Happy Hauntings" was stitched on café mocha 32-count country French linen by Wichelt using DMC floss and Kreinik blending filament. Finished piece was custom framed.

Skill Level

*Easy

Stitch Count

97 wide x 75 high

Approximate Design Size

11-count 8⅞" x 6⅞"
14-count 7" x 5⅜"
16-count 6" x 4⅝"
18-count 5⅜" x 4⅛"
22-count 4⅜" x 3⅜"
32-count over 2 threads 6" x 4⅝"

Instructions

1. For framed piece, center and stitch design on linen, stitching over two threads and using two strands floss or two strands floss and one strand blending filament for Cross-Stitch, two strands floss for Straight Stitch, and one strand floss for Lazy-Daisy Stitch, Backstitch and French Knot.

2. For card, stitch center portion of design on black plastic canvas, using three strands floss or two strands floss and one strand blending filament for Cross-Stitch, and two strands floss for Backstitch. **Note:** *When stitching "Fright Night," use white floss for portions of lettering directly on black plastic canvas; use dark charcoal for portions of lettering overlapping moon, as graphed.*

3. Cut plastic canvas one hole beyond stitching. Cut a piece of double-stick adhesive sheet to fit plastic canvas; remove paper backing from one side of adhesive sheet and apply to back of stitched piece. Remove paper backing from remaining side of adhesive sheet and adhere to purple card stock; trim purple card stock to fit. Apply stitched unit to piece of yellow corrugated paper in same manner. Fold 10- x 7-inch piece of blue card stock in half to make a 5- x 7-inch card; adhere yellow corrugated paper to lower right-hand corner of card front. Use alphabet stickers to spell "Boo To You!" or desired sentiment on front of card.

4. For magnet, stitch far-right portion of design on black plastic canvas, using three strands floss or two strands floss and one strand blending filament for Cross-Stitch, and two strands floss for Backstitch. **Note:** *Use white to Backstitch lettering.* Cut plastic canvas one hole beyond stitching. Using fabric glue, attach black felt to back of stitched piece; trim to fit. Glue stitched unit to green felt; trim green felt, leaving ⅛-inch border. Attach magnet strips to back of green felt. ❖

CROSS-STITCH (2X)

ANCHOR		DMC	COLORS
2	·	White	White
400	✳	317	Pewter gray
215	□	320	Medium pistachio green
217	♣	367	Dark pistachio green
1047	／	402	Very light mahogany
236	％	413	Dark pewter gray
235	▣	414	Dark steel gray
903	?	640	Very dark beige gray
392	○	642	Dark beige gray
830	┃	644	Medium beige gray
305	◇	725	Topaz
890	★	729	Medium old gold
1012	♡	754	Light peach
944	▤	869	Very dark hazelnut brown
1003	◤	921	Copper
1003	✖	922	Light copper
1011	⌐	948	Very light peach
260	m	3364	Pine green
236	▲	3799	Very dark pewter gray

KREINIK BLENDED CROSS-STITCH

ANCHOR		DMC	COLORS
2	I	White	White* (2X) with 100 white BF (1X)
293	◁	727	Very light topaz (2X) with 091 star yellow BF (1X)
392	∩	3078	Very light golden yellow (2X) with 091 star yellow* BF (1X)
236	✿	3799	Very dark pewter gray* (2X) with 005 black BF (1X)

LAZY-DAISY STITCH (1X)

ANCHOR		DMC	COLOR
236	—	3799	Very dark pewter gray*

STRAIGHT STITCH (2X)

ANCHOR		DMC	COLOR
890	—	729	Medium old gold*

BACKSTITCH (1X)

ANCHOR		DMC	COLORS
217	—	367	Dark pistachio green*
236	—	3799	Very dark pewter gray*

FRENCH KNOT (1X)

ANCHOR		DMC	COLOR
236	●	3799	Very dark pewter gray*

Lazy-Daisy Stitch

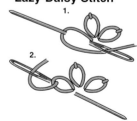

Happy Halloween

Design by Lois Winston

Stir up a batch of Halloween fun! Add pumpkin flavor to your kitchen decor, then cuddle up for cooler weather with a warm sweatshirt.

Materials
- Towel with 12-count Aida border
- 14-count Waste Canvas
- Sweatshirt
- Interfacing

"Happy Halloween" projects were stitched on a Crafter's Pride Milano Waffle Weave Towel by Daniel Enterprises, using DMC floss.

Skill Level
**Average

Stitch Count
127 wide x 23 high

Approximate Design Size
11-count 11⅝" x 2⅛"
12-count 10⅝" x 2"
14-count 9⅛" x 1¾"
16-count 8" x 1½"
18-count 7⅛" x 1⅜"
22-count 5⅞" x 1⅛"

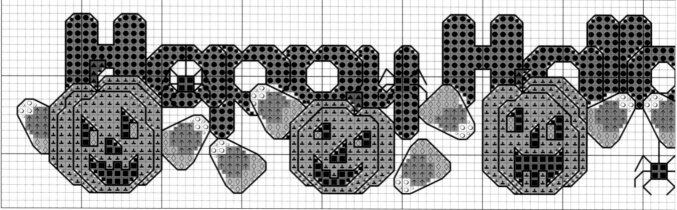

Instructions

1. For towel, center and stitch design onto Aida border using two strands floss for Cross-Stitch, and one strand floss for Backstitch.

2. For sweatshirt, position and baste interfacing to wrong side of sweatshirt; next, apply Waste Canvas to front of sweatshirt. Center and stitch design using two strands floss for Cross-Stitch and one strand floss for Backstitch. Remove Waste Canvas after stitching. Trim interfacing close to stitching. ❖

Tip!

For stitching "Happy Halloween" on a dark fabric like the sweatshirt shown, substitute DMC 414 steel gray for DMC 310 black.

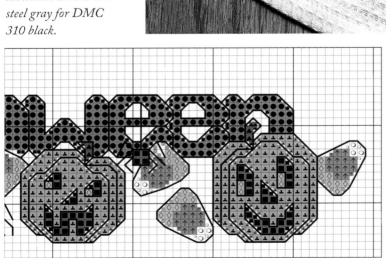

CROSS-STITCH (2X)

ANCHOR	DMC		COLORS
2	○	White	White
110	●	208	Very dark lavender
403	■	310	Black
358	▲	433	Medium brown
304	⊥	741	Medium tangerine
316	↑	970	Light pumpkin
297	◇	973	Bright canary

BACKSTITCH (1X)

ANCHOR	DMC		COLOR
403	—	310	Black*

*Duplicate color

Boo! Tote

Design by Carolyn Manning

Your little ghostie will love collecting treats in this tote bag.

Remove the buttons if the bag becomes soiled for easy laundering!

Materials

- White 14-count Aida: 9½ x 9½ inches
- Mill Hill ceramic buttons: trick-or-treat boy #86032B, trick-or-treat girl #86032G, trick-or-treat pumpkin #86033, ghost #86024, witch #86025 and bat #86026
- 17 x 13-inch black canvas tote bag

"Boo! Tote" was stitched on white 14-count Aida using DMC floss.

Skill Level

*Easy

Stitch Count

77 wide x 76 high

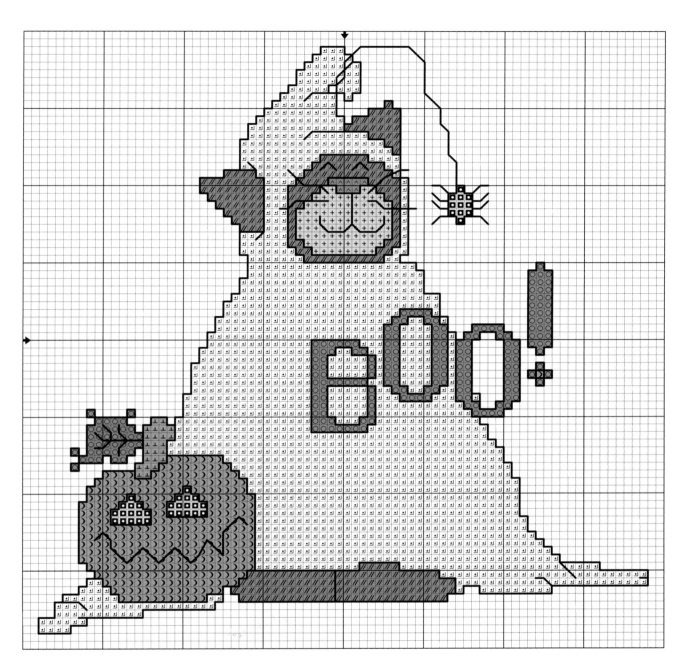

Approximate Design Size

11-count 7" x 7"
14-count 5½" x 5½"
16-count 4¾" x 4¾"
18-count 4¼" x 4¼"
22-count 3½" x 3½"

Instructions

1. Center and stitch design on Aida using three strands floss for Cross-Stitch, and two strands floss for Backstitch.

Finishing

1. Turn raw edges under ¼ inch; turn under again ½ inch. Hand- or machine-stitch hem in place.

2. Sew pumpkin, witch, ghost and bat buttons in corners of stitched panel to secure to tote bag. Sew trick-or-treat boy and girl buttons to top of bag just below handle ends. ❖

CROSS-STITCH (3X)

ANCHOR		DMC	COLORS
403	▣	310	Black
235	▨	414	Dark steel gray
398	+	415	Pearl gray
310	⊥	434	Light brown
326	◗	720	Dark orange spice
268	◯	937	Medium avocado green
38	∧	3832	Medium raspberry
2	⅃	3865	Winter white

BACKSTITCH (2X)

ANCHOR		DMC	COLOR
403	—	310	Black*

*Duplicate color

Horn of Plenty

Design by Pamela Kellogg

Create a focal point for your dining room with this lovely cornucopia.

Worked on 14–count Aida, minimal backstitching adds depth to the realistic shading.

Materials

- Ivory 14-count Aida:
  20 x 18 inches

"Horn of Plenty" was stitched on ivory 14-count Aida by Zweigart using DMC floss. Finished piece was custom framed.

Skill Level

**Average

Stitch Count

167 wide x 136 high

Approximate Design Size

11-count 15⅛" x 12⅜"
14-count 11⅞" x 9⅝"
16-count 10½" x 8½"
18-count 9¼" x 7½"
22-count 7⅝" x 6⅛"

Instructions

1. Center and stitch design, using three strands floss for Cross-Stitch and one strand floss for Backstitch. ❖

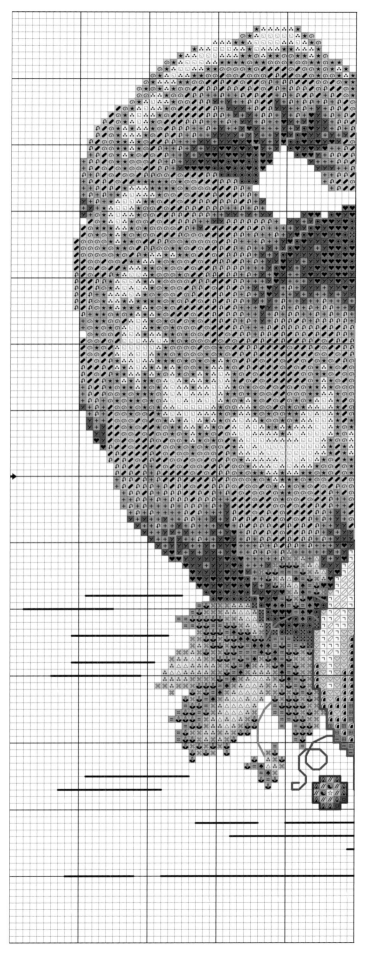

CROSS-STITCH (3X)

ANCHOR		DMC	COLORS
2	·	White	White
1049	–	301	Medium mahogany
1006	<	304	Medium red
9046	⊞	321	Red
351	▨	400	Dark mahogany
358	Y	433	Medium brown
310	+	434	Light brown
1046	∩	435	Very light brown
1045	◢	436	Tan
362	⌐	437	Light tan
267	⊁	469	Avocado green
266	◖	470	Light avocado green
265	✕	471	Very light avocado green
253	⊥	472	Ultra light avocado green
1005	«	498	Dark red
46	✳	666	Bright red
926	▣	712	Cream
361	★	738	Very light tan
387	∴	739	Ultra very light tan
300	⌐	745	Light pale yellow
275	⊘	746	Off-white
259	△	772	Very light yellow green
133	■	796	Dark royal blue
132	☐	797	Royal blue
131	◮	798	Dark Delft blue
136	⫽	799	Medium Delft blue
144	☆	800	Pale Delft blue
359	♥	801	Dark coffee brown
130	☜	809	Delft blue
43	∩	815	Medium garnet
20	✳	816	Garnet
134	╬	820	Very dark royal blue
1044	◆	895	Very dark hunter green
360	⊙	898	Very dark coffee brown
861	▤	935	Dark avocado green
269	○	936	Very dark avocado green
268	⊠	937	Medium avocado green
381	⊠	938	Ultra dark coffee brown
268	═	3345	Dark hunter green
267	⬇	3346	Hunter green
266	⌘	3347	Medium yellow green
264	⁖	3348	Light yellow green
35	☐	3705	Dark melon
33	�	3706	Medium melon
31	∷	3708	Light melon
35	⋈	3801	Very dark melon
1003	⊞	3853	Dark autumn gold
1002	◖	3854	Medium autumn gold
301	♡	3855	Light autumn gold

BLENDED CROSS-STITCH

ANCHOR		DMC	COLOR
351	◥	400	Dark mahogany* (2X) with 1049/ 301 medium mahogany* (1X)

BACKSTITCH (1X)

ANCHOR		DMC	COLORS
351	▬	400	Dark mahogany* (pumpkins)
1046	▬	435	Very light brown*
45	▬	814	Dark garnet (apple)
134	▬	820	Very dark royal blue* (grapes)
1044	▬	895	Very dark hunter green* (pumpkin leaves)
861	▬	935	Dark avocado green* (grape leaves and curlicues)
382	▬	3371	Black brown

*Duplicate color

CROSS-STITCH (3X)

ANCHOR		DMC	COLORS
2	·	White	White
1049	−	301	Medium mahogany
1006	<	304	Medium red
9046	⋕	321	Red
351	▨	400	Dark mahogany
358	Y	433	Medium brown
310	+	434	Light brown
1046	⋂	435	Very light brown
1045	◢	436	Tan
362	ଗ	437	Light tan
267	⊬	469	Avocado green
266	◖	470	Light avocado green
265	X	471	Very light avocado green
253	⊥	472	Ultra light avocado green
1005	«	498	Dark red
46	✳	666	Bright red
926	⊡	712	Cream
361	★	738	Very light tan
387	∴	739	Ultra very light tan
300	⌐	745	Light pale yellow
275	⊘	746	Off-white
259	△	772	Very light yellow green
133	■	796	Dark royal blue
132	▢	797	Royal blue
131	◭	798	Dark Delft blue
136	//	799	Medium Delft blue
144	☆	800	Pale Delft blue
359	▼	801	Dark coffee brown
130	◐	809	Delft blue
43	∏	815	Medium garnet
20	✳	816	Garnet
134	⊞	820	Very dark royal blue
1044	♠	895	Very dark hunter green
360	◉	898	Very dark coffee brown
861	▣	935	Dark avocado green
269	o	936	Very dark avocado green
268	⊠	937	Medium avocado green
381	⋈	938	Ultra dark coffee brown
268	=	3345	Dark hunter green
267	⬇	3346	Hunter green
266	⌘	3347	Medium yellow green
264	✲	3348	Light yellow green
35	▢	3705	Dark melon
33	⅃	3706	Medium melon
31	∷	3708	Light melon
35	⋈	3801	Very dark melon
1003	⊞	3853	Dark autumn gold
1002	◪	3854	Medium autumn gold
301	♡	3855	Light autumn gold

BLENDED CROSS-STITCH

ANCHOR		DMC	COLOR
351	◣	400	Dark mahogany* (2X) with 1049/ 301 medium mahogany* (1X)

BACKSTITCH (1X)

ANCHOR		DMC	COLORS
351	▬	400	Dark mahogany* (pumpkins)
1046	▬	435	Very light brown*
45	▬	814	Dark garnet (apple)
134	▬	820	Very dark royal blue* (grapes)
1044	▬	895	Very dark hunter green* (pumpkin leaves)
861	▬	935	Dark avocado green* (grape leaves and curlicues)
382	▬	3371	Black brown

*Duplicate color

Be Thou Thankful

Design by Susan Stadler

Stitch this "sampler" as a reminder to be thankful for simple things!

Materials
- Beige 14-count Aida: 13½ x 13½ inches
- ¾-inch-diameter brass sun charm
- Beige all-purpose thread

"Be Thou Thankful" was stitched on beige 14-count Aida by Charles Craft using floss from DMC and Weeks Dye Works. Finished piece was custom framed.

Skill Level
*Easy

Stitch Count
79 wide x 79 high

Approximate Design Size
11-count 7⅛" x 7⅛"
14-count 5⅝" x 5⅝"
16-count 5" x 5"
18-count 4⅜" x 4⅜"
22-count 3⅝" x 3⅝"

Instructions
1. Center and stitch design, stitching over one square using three strands floss for Cross-Stitch and one or two strands for Backstitch and Straight Stitch.

2. Use alphabet and numerical graph to personalize as desired with initials and date.

3. Attach sun charm with beige all-purpose thread above wheat shock. ❖

CROSS-STITCH (3X)

ANCHOR		DMC	COLORS
387	♡	Ecru	Ecru
897	◐	221	Very dark shell pink
403	◨	310	Black
374	⋔	420	Dark hazelnut brown
861	❖	935	Dark avocado green
881	~	945	Tawny
295	∷	3822	Light straw

DMC		WEEKS DYE WORKS	COLORS
779	╱	1270	Rum raisin
3362	◆	2200	Kudzu
920	◄	2239	Terra cotta

BACKSTITCH (1X)

DMC		WEEKS DYE WORKS	COLORS
779	—	1270	Rum raisin*

BACKSTITCH/ STRAIGHT STITCH (2X)

ANCHOR		DMC	COLORS
403	—	310	Black*
295	—	3822	Light straw*

*Duplicate color

Thanksgiving Decor

Designs by Lois Winston

Stitch these motifs on a napkin, place mat or basket band. Use the same motifs to create

matching napkin rings and coasters—the possibilities are endless!

Materials

- 3-inch-wide 22-count linen stitch band: desired length
- Prefinished white 14-count place mat: 18 x 13 inches
- Graph paper
- Colored pencils or markers
- Prefinished white 14-count napkin: 15 x 15 inches
- Basket
- Craft glue or hot-glue gun

"Thanksgiving Decor" was stitched on white 14-count place mat #RC-4851-6750 and white 14-count napkin #RC-4852-6750 from Charles Craft.

Skill Level

**Average

Stitch Count

122 wide x 22 high

Approximate Design Size

11-count 11⅛" x 2"
14-count 8¾" x 1½"
16-count 7⅝" x 1⅜"

18-count 6¾" x 1¼"
22-count 5½" x 1"
22-count over two threads 11⅛" x 2"

Instructions

1. For basket trim, center and stitch design on 22-count stitch band, stitching over two threads using two strands floss for Cross-Stitch and one strand floss for Backstitch.

2. For 14-count place mat and napkin, select desired motifs from graph and chart onto graph paper for proper placement. *Note: There should be 1 inch between design and fringe.* Center and stitch design of choice onto corner of place mat or napkin using two strands floss for Cross-Stitch and one strand floss for Backstitch.

Finishing

1. Position stitch band around basket as desired and glue in place. ❖

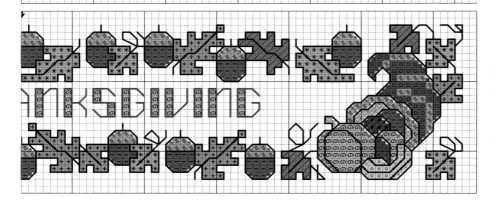

CROSS-STITCH (2X)

ANCHOR		DMC	COLORS
100	◕	327	Dark violet
1046	▫	435	Very light brown
362	↳	437	Light tan
266	▬	470	Light avocado green
326	◎	720	Dark orange spice
890	+	729	Medium old gold
359	♡	801	Dark coffee brown
20	≪	816	Garnet
1003	╱	921	Copper
1002	✳	3854	Medium autumn gold
301	○	3855	Light autumn gold

BACKSTITCH (1X)

ANCHOR		DMC	COLORS
403	—	310	Black
359	—	801	Dark coffee brown*

*Duplicate color

Holiday Duo

Designs by Ursula Michael

Decorate your kitchen in seasonal motifs with

these projects that are functional as well as pretty.

Materials

- Two ecru Showcase kitchen towels with 4½ x 6-inch 14-count Aida inserts
- Ecru pot holder with 5 x 7-inch 14-count Aida insert
- Graph paper

"Holiday Duo" was stitched on Showcase Huck Towel HF-6500–2724-EA ecru and Kitchen Mate Pot Holder #PH-6201-2724-EA by Charles Craft using DMC floss.

Skill Level

*Easy

Pumpkin
Stitch Count

54 wide x 67 high

Approximate Design Size

11-count 5" x 6⅛"
14-count 3⅞" x 4⅞"

16-count 3⅜" x 4¼"
18-count 3" x 3¾"
22-count 2½" x 3⅛"

Give Thanks
Stitch Count
52 wide x 71 high

Approximate Design Size
11-count 4¾" x 6½"
14-count 3¾" x 5⅛"
16-count 3¼" x 4½"
18-count 3" x 4"
22-count 2⅜" x 3¼"

Instructions

1. For towel, center and stitch design of choice onto towel insert using two strands floss for Cross-Stitch and one strand floss for Backstitch.

2. For pot holder, center and stitch design of choice onto insert, using two strands floss for Cross-Stitch and one strand floss for Backstitch. ❖

Pumpkin
CROSS-STITCH (2X)

ANCHOR		DMC	COLORS
1044	4	895	Very dark hunter green
333	◆◆	900	Dark burnt orange
340	#	918	Dark red copper
330	$	947	Burnt orange
244	⁒	987	Dark forest green
242	L	989	Forest green
323	○	3825	Pale pumpkin

Pumpkin

Give Thanks

CROSS-STITCH (2X)

ANCHOR		DMC	COLORS
893	L	224	Very light shell pink
1026	∞	225	Ultra very light shell pink
891	$	676	Light old gold
890	#	729	Medium old gold
1044	∙∙	895	Very dark hunter green
333	%	900	Dark burnt orange
341	⊥	918	Dark red copper
355	◢	975	Dark golden brown
244	)	987	Dark forest green
242	✳	989	forest green
1027	+	3722	Medium shell pink
323	↑	3825	Pale pumpkin
901	·	3829	Very dark old gold

BACKSTITCH (1X)

ANCHOR		DMC	COLOR
1005	—	816	Garnet

Santa's Cup of Tea

Design by Gail Bussi

Keep your Earl Grey, oolong and black pekoe teabags fresh and ready to add to hot water.

You never know when Santa will be by to join you in a cup!

Materials

- Flax 32-count Belfast linen:
  13½ x 13½ inches
- Square wooden box with 6x6-inch
  design insert area
- Polyester or cotton quilt batting

"Santa's Cup of Tea" was stitched on flax 32-count Belfast linen by Zweigart using DMC floss. Finished piece was inserted in simply square box #99731 from Sudberry House.

Skill Level

**Average

Stitch Count

97 wide x 97 high

Approximate Design Size

11-count 8⅞" x 8⅞"
14-count 7" x 7"
16-count 6" x 6"
18-count 5⅜" x 5⅜"
22-count 4⅜" x 4⅜"
32-count over two threads 6" x 6"

Instructions

1. Center and stitch design, stitching
over two threads and using two strands
floss for Cross-Stitch, and one strand
floss for Backstitch, French Knot
and Eyelet Stitch. (See Eyelet Stitch
illustration on page 141.)

2. Insert in box opening following
manufacturer's direction. *Note: Pad
top of box with two layers of polyester or
cotton quilt batting so checked border of
design will show through opening.* ❖

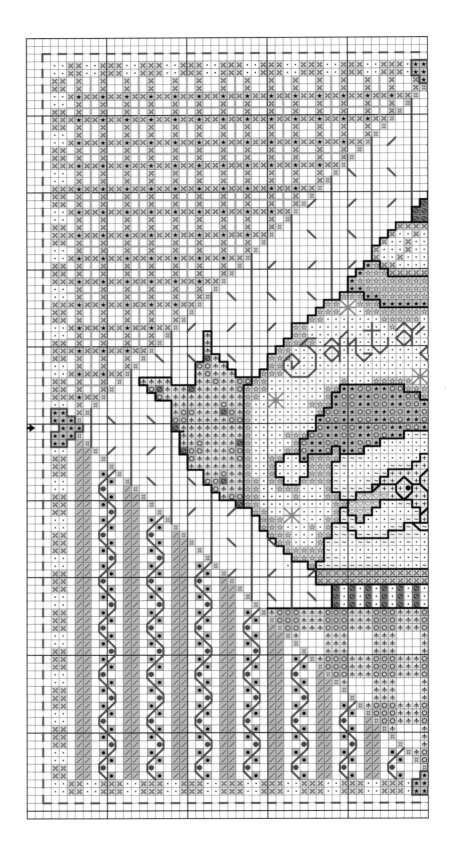

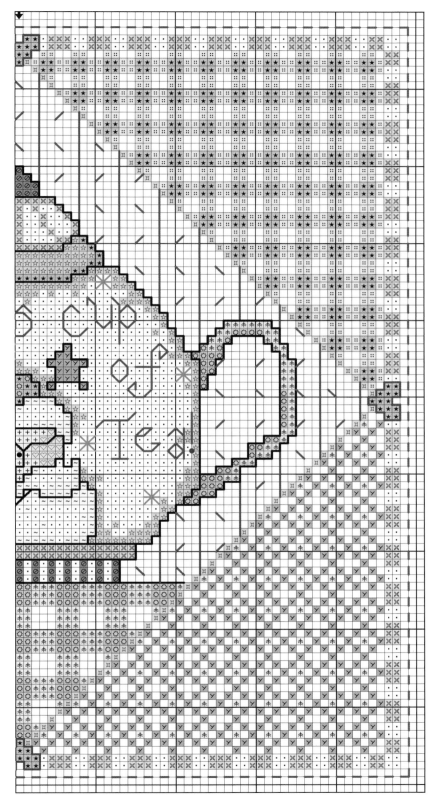

CROSS-STITCH (2X)

ANCHOR		DMC	COLORS
2	·	White	White
1025	⊘	347	Very dark salmon
6	♡	353	Peach
878	✿	501	Dark blue green
877	✖	502	Blue green
891	⅄	676	Light old gold
886	⊞	677	Very light old gold
1022	∷	760	Medium salmon pink
234	~	762	Very light pearl gray
390	☆	822	Light beige gray
1011	+	948	Very light peach
1024	★	3328	Dark Salmon
1023	∕	3712	Medium salmon
877	●	3815	Dark celadon green
8785	朩	3817	Light celadon green

EYELET STITCH (1X)

ANCHOR		DMC	COLOR
890	▬	729	Medium old gold

BACKSTITCH (1X)

ANCHOR		DMC	COLORS
1025	▬	347	Very dark salmon*
878	▬	501	Dark blue green*
890	▬	729	Medium old gold*
236	▬	3799	Very dark pewter gray

FRENCH KNOT (1X)

ANCHOR		DMC	COLORS
1025	●	347	Very dark salmon*
878	●	501	Dark blue green*
236	●	3799	Very dark pewter gray*

*Duplicate color

Christmas Goodies Bellpull

Design by Lois Winston

Sweet treats on a narrow band will add holiday cheer to hard-to-decorate spots in your home.

Materials

- White 3-inch-wide 14-count stitch band with gold trim: 16 inches in length
- Kreinik #8 fine braid: silver #001 and gold #002
- 2 bellpull's hardware with 3-inch middle
- White backing fabric: 4 x 16 inches (optional)

"Christmas Goodies Bellpull" was stitched using DMC floss.

Skill Level

*Easy

Stitch Count

25 wide x 164 high

Approximate Design Size

11-count 2¼" x 15"
14-count 1¾" x 11⅝"
16-count 1½" x 10¼"
18-count 1⅜" x 9"
22-count 1⅛" x 7½"

Instructions

1. Center and stitch design on stitch band using two strands floss or one strand fine braid for Cross-Stitch and one strand floss for Backstitch.

Finishing

1. Cut stitch band at desired length and attach to bellpull's hardware following manufacturer's instructions.

2. If desired, apply backing to bellpull by turning under raw edges of backing fabric and whipstitching edges to bellpull. ❖

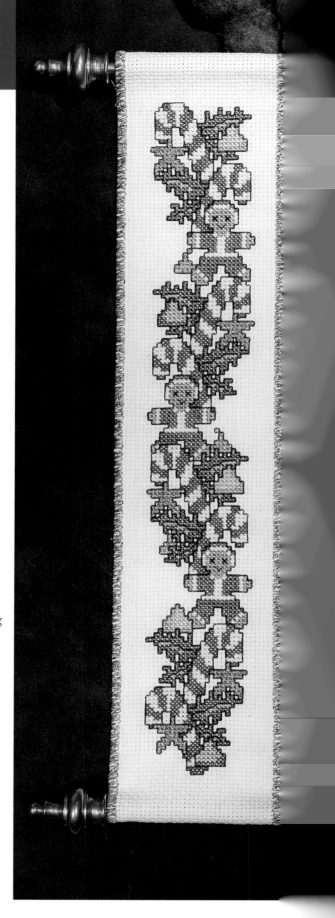

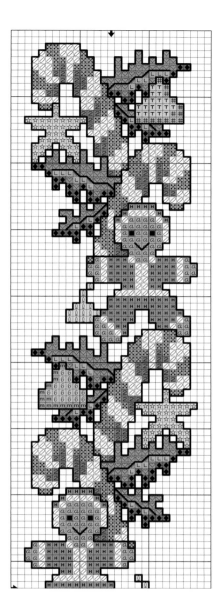
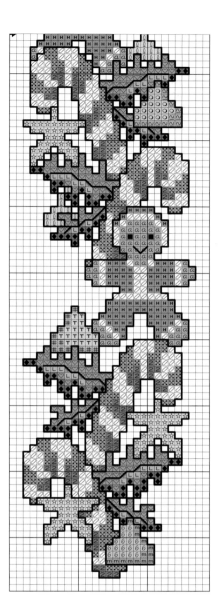

CROSS-STITCH (2X)

ANCHOR		DMC	COLORS
1	⬭	White	White
1006	2	304	Medium red
403	■	310	Black
9046	✕	321	Red
1045	a	436	Tan
878	◆	501	Dark blue green
99	m	552	Medium violet
96	6	554	Very light violet
316	≈	740	Tangerine
303	O	742	Light tangerine
40	#	956	Geranium
50	T	957	Pale geranium
877	♡	3815	Dark celadon green
875	L	3817	Light celadon green
189	H	3850	Dark bright green

CROSS-STITCH (1X)

KREINIK #8 BRAID		COLORS
001	⬭	Silver
002	☆	Gold

BACKSTITCH (1X)

ANCHOR		DMC	COLOR
403	—	310	Black*

*Duplicate color

Holiday Helper

Design by Ursula Michael

A wreath with a big bow will look festive while you dry dishes after a winter meal.

Materials
- White Showcase kitchen towel with a 4½ x 6-inch 14-count Aida insert

"Holiday Helper" was stitched on Showcase Huck Towel #HF-6500-6750-EA white by Charles Craft using DMC floss.

Skill Level
*Easy

Stitch Count
52 wide x 71 high

Approximate Design Size
11-count 4¾" x 5⅝"
14-count 3¾" x 4⅜"
16-count 3¼" x 3⅞"
18-count 3" x 3⅜"
22-count 2⅜" x 2⅞"

Instructions
1. Center and stitch design on towel insert using two strands floss for Cross-Stitch, and one strand floss for Backstitch. ❖

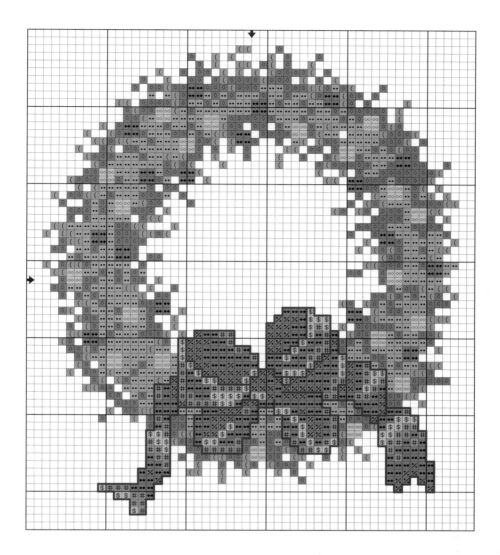

Cross-Stitch (2X)

ANCHOR		DMC	COLORS
9046	◆◆	321	Red
11	#	350	Medium coral
9	$	352	Light coral
1005	%	816	Garnet
1044	••	895	Very dark hunter green
244	◊	987	Dark forest green
242	(	989	Forest green
701	∞	5282	Gold metallic

BackStitch (1X)

ANCHOR		DMC	COLOR
1005	—	816	Garnet*

*Duplicate color

Country Charm Ornament Bags

Designs by Hope Murphy

You'll be able to make a batch of these little ornament bags

in no time at all, thanks to prefinished stitchband!

Smyrna Cross

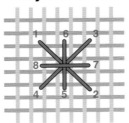

Materials
- Raw linen 22-count stitchband #7272/053: 1 yard
- 4 (12-inch) lengths jute twine for handles
- Pinking shears

"Country Charm Ornament Bags" were stitched on raw linen 22-count stitchband by Zweigart using DMC floss.

Skill Level
*Easy

Flag
Stitch Count
24 wide x 32 high

Approximate Design Size
11-count 2⅛" x 3"
14-count 1¾" x 2¼"
16-count 1½" x 2"
18-count 1⅜" x 1¾"
22-count 1" x 1½"

Heart
Stitch Count
26 wide x 25 high heart

Approximate Design Size
11-count 2⅜" x 2¼"
14-count 1⅞" x 1¾"
16-count 1⅝" x 1½"
18-count 1½" x 1⅜"
22-count 1" x 1⅛"

Stocking
Stitch Count
28 wide x 29 high

Approximate Design Size
11-count 2½" x 2⅝"
14-count 2 x 2⅛"

16-count 1¾" x 1⅞"
18-count 1½" x 1⅝"
22-count 1¼" x 1⅜"

Tree
Stitch Count
22 wide x 24 high

Approximate Design Size
11-count 2" x 2⅛"
14-count 1½" x 1¾"
16-count 1⅜" x 1½"
18-count 1¼" x 1⅜"
22-count 1" x 1⅛"

Instructions

1. Use pinking shears to cut stitchband into four equal lengths. Fold each piece in half; press. Fold down each raw edge 1 inch to form cuff; press.

2. Unfold each piece; center and stitch design on front side of stitchband below cuff, stitching over two threads using four strands floss for Cross-Stitch and Smyrna Cross-Stitch and two strands floss for Backstitch. *Note: For stocking only, work Backstitching over one thread, referring to separate graph and beginning at black dot on stocking graph.*

Finishing

1. Knot each length of jute twine approximately ½ inch from end for handles.

2. Refold stitchband. Position jute handle inside stitchband just below bottom cuff line with ends extending from edges.

3. With four strands of contrasting floss, stitch sides of stitchband together with a running stitch, catching jute handle between layers. Pull handle through top of bag to draw knotted ends close to stitching. ❖

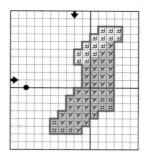

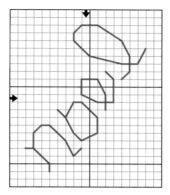

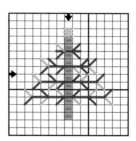

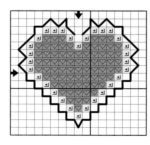

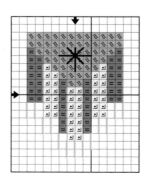

Stocking–Noel

CROSS-STITCH (4X)

ANCHOR		DMC	COLORS
387	◢	Ecru	Ecru
262	▦	3052	Medium green gray
29	⅄	3831	Dark raspberry

BACKSTITCH (2X)

ANCHOR		DMC	COLORS
862	—	520	Dark fern green
29	—	3831	Dark raspberry*

*Duplicate color

Tree

CROSS-STITCH (4X)

ANCHOR		DMC	COLOR
1086	∞	839	Dark beige brown

SMYRNA CROSS-STITCH (4X)

ANCHOR		DMC	COLORS
890	⬭	729	Medium old gold

BACKSTITCH (2X)

ANCHOR		DMC	COLORS
862	—	520	Dark fern green
360	—	839	Dark beige brown*
262	—	3052	Medium green gray

*Duplicate color

Heart

CROSS-STITCH (4X)

ANCHOR		DMC	COLORS
387	◢	Ecru	Ecru
39	♡	3831	Dark raspberry

BACKSTITCH (2X)

ANCHOR		DMC	COLOR
387	—	Ecru	Ecru*

*Duplicate color

Flag

CROSS-STITCH (4X)

ANCHOR		DMC	COLORS
387	◢	Ecru	Ecru
978	↘	322	Dark dark baby blue
39	=	3831	Dark raspberry

BACKSTITCH (2X)

ANCHOR		DMC	COLORS
387	—	Ecru	Ecru*
890	—	729	Medium old gold

*Duplicate color

Snowman and Friends

Design by Carole Rodgers

Ceramic buttons add dimension to a very dapper winter snowman.

CROSS-STITCH (3X)

ANCHOR	DMC		COLORS
2	③	White	White
1049	••	301	Medium mahogany
403	↑	310	Black
398	⊗⊗	415	Pearl gray
43	$	815	Medium garnet
268	⫽	3345	Dark hunter green

BACKSTITCH (2X)

ANCHOR	DMC		COLOR
403	—	310	Black*

FRENCH KNOT (2X)

ANCHOR	DMC		COLORS
403	●	310	Black* (eyes)
330	●	947	Burnt orange (nose)

ATTACHMENT (2X)

ANCHOR	DMC		COLORS
	●		Red bird button
	●		Penguin button

*Duplicate color

Materials
- Natural 10-count Heatherfield: 9 x 9 inches
- Mill Hill ceramic buttons: penguin #86146 and red bird #86175

"Snowman & Friends" was stitched on natural 10-count Heatherfield by Wichelt Imports Inc. using DMC floss. Finished piece was custom framed.

Skill Level
*Easy

Stitch Count
37 wide x 38 high

Approximate Design Size
10-count 3¾" x 3⅞"
11-count 3⅜" x 3½"
14-count 2¾" x 2¾"
16-count 2⅜" x 2⅜"
18-count 2⅛" x 2⅛"
22-count 1¾" x 1¾"

Instructions
1. Center and stitch design using three strands floss for Cross-Stitch and two strands floss for Backstitch and French Knot.

2. Use two strands coordinating floss for securing buttons according to graph. ❖

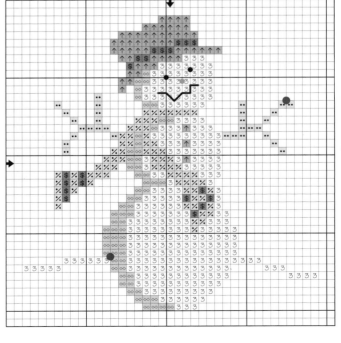

Santa Sampler

Design by Lois Winston

Bordered with holly, these non-traditional Santas give a new look to this year's holiday season!

Materials
- Antique white 14-count Aida:
  12 x 14 inches

"Santa Sampler" was stitched on antique white 14-count Aida by Zweigart using DMC floss. Finished piece was custom framed.

Skill Level
**Average

Stitch Count
89 wide x 113 high

Approximate Design Size
11-count 8" x 10¼"
14-count 6⅜" x 8"
16-count 5½" x 7"
18-count 5" x 6¼"
22-count 4" x 5⅛"

Instructions
1. Center and stitch design on 14-count Aida, using three strands floss for Cross-Stitch and one strand floss for Backstitch. Use three strands floss for French Knot, wrapping needle twice. ❖

CROSS-STITCH (3X)

ANCHOR		DMC	COLORS
403	▫	310	Black
1025	♦	347	Very dark salmon
1005	◪	498	Dark red
878	⌘	501	Dark blue green
1042	−	504	Very light blue green
926	V	712	Cream
890	✿	729	Medium old gold
1080	◎	842	Very light beige brown
4146	▫	950	Light desert sand
852	∷	3047	Light yellow beige
1028	◣	3685	Very dark mauve
876	H	3816	Celadon green
29	Y	3831	Dark raspberry
26	☆	3833	Light raspberry
1076	O	3847	Dark teal green
1047	⊞	3848	Medium teal green
1070	X	3849	Light teal green
307	✳	3852	Very dark straw
379	♣	3860	Cocoa
2	◙	3865	Winter white
926	~	3866	Ultra very light mocha beige

BACKSTITCH (1X)

ANCHOR		DMC	COLOR
403	—	310	Black*

FRENCH KNOT (3X)

ANCHOR		DMC	COLOR
403	●	310	Black* (eyes)

*Duplicate color

Jewel-Tone Ornaments

Design by Lois Winston

Whether you choose to stitch these in traditional colors using metallic braids or stitch the version

with Mexican-inspired hues, you'll love how these ornaments look on your tree!

Materials

- 2 sheets 14-count plastic canvas
- 2 yards gold nonravel 2mm bead trim (optional finishing for metallic ornaments)
- ⅝-inch gold jingle bell (optional finishing for metallic ornaments)
- Red and white jingle bells in sizes ranging from ⅜-inch to ½-inch (optional finishing for floss ornaments)

"Jewel-Tone Ornaments" were stitched using Anchor floss for floss ornaments and Kreinik #4 and #8 braids for the metallic ornaments.

Skill Level

**Average

Star Ornament Stitch Count

47 wide x 49 high

Approximate Design Size

11-count 4¼" x 4½"
14-count 3⅜" x 3½"
16-count 2⅞" x 3"
18-count 2⅝" x 2¾"
22-count 2⅛" x 2¼"

Oblong Ornament Stitch Count

33 wide x 49 high

Approximate Design Size

11-count 3" x 4½"
14-count 2⅜" x 3½"
16-count 2" x 3"
18-count 1⅞" x 2¾"
22-count 1½" x 2¼"

Round Ornament Stitch Count

45 wide x 49 high

Approximate Design Size

11-count 4" x 4½"
14-count 3¼" x 3½"
16-count 2¾" x 3"
18-count 2½" x 2¾"
22-count 2" x 2¼"

Bell Ornament Stitch Count

47 wide x 49 high

Approximate Design Size

11-count 4¼" x 4½"
14-count 3⅜" x 3½"
16-count 2⅞" x 3"
18-count 2⅝" x 2¾"
22-count 2⅛" x 2¼"

Instructions

1. Center and stitch design, stitching over one thread using three strands floss or one strand braid for Cross-Stitch, and one strand floss or braid for Backstitch.

Finishing

1. Trim plastic canvas one hole beyond stitching.

2. For each ornament, cut an 8-inch strand of braid or floss; glue both ends to the top back of ornament to form a hanging loop.

3. Glue each ornament to felt; let dry. Trim felt to fit ornament.

Optional Finishing

1. For metallic ornaments, couch nonravel gold bead trim to outside edges of each ornament. Attach gold jingle bell to bottom center of bell ornament.

2. For floss ornaments, attach jingle bells as desired. ❖

Star Ornament

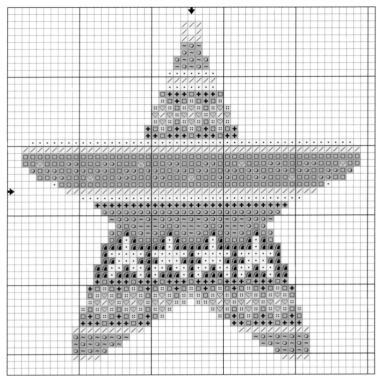

Metallic Color Key

CROSS-STITCH (1X)

KREINIK #8 BRAID		COLORS
002HL	⟋	Gold hi lustre
003HL	♡	Red hi lustre
008HL	◯	Green hi lustre
009HL	✕	Emerald hi lustre
012HL	✚	Purple hi lustre
032	·	Pearl
051HL	☐	Sapphire hi lustre
061	～	Ruby
094	∷	Star blue
308	◨	Colonial red

BACKSTITCH (1X)

KREINIK #4 BRAID		COLOR
032	━	Pearl*

*Duplicate color

Floss Color Key

CROSS-STITCH (3X)

DMC		ANCHOR	COLORS
444	⟋	290	Dark lemon
3705	♡	35	Dark melon
905	◯	257	Dark parrot
986	✕	246	Very d
327	✚	100	D
White	·	2	
995	☐	410	
666	～		
996			

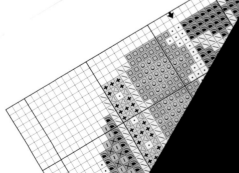

Bell Ornament

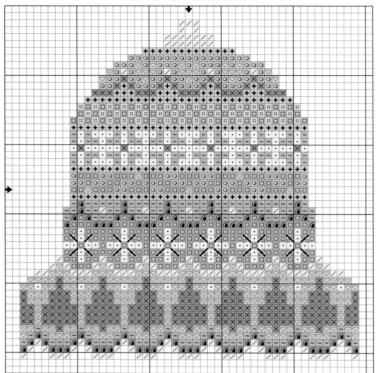

Metallic Color Key

CROSS-STITCH (1X)

KREINIK #8 BRAID		COLORS
002HL	╱	Gold hi lustre
003HL	♡	Red hi lustre
008HL	⊙	Green hi lustre
009HL	✕	Emerald hi lustre
012HL	✚	Purple hi lustre
032	·	Pearl
051HL	▫	Sapphire hi lustre
061	~	Ruby
094	⠿	Star blue
308	◩	Colonial red

BACKSTITCH (1X)

KREINIK #4 BRAID		COLOR
032	▬	Pearl*

*Duplicate color

Floss Color Key

CROSS-STITCH (3X)

DMC	ANCHOR		COLORS
444	╱	290	Dark lemon
3705	♡	35	Dark melon
905	⊙	257	Dark parrot green
986	✕	246	Very dark forest green
327	✚	100	Dark violet
White	·	2	White
995	▫	410	Dark electric blue
666	~	46	Bright red
996	⠿	433	Medium electric blue
321	◩	9046	Red

BACKSTITCH (1X)

DMC	ANCHOR	COLOR
White	▬ 2	White*

*Duplicate color

Oblong Ornament

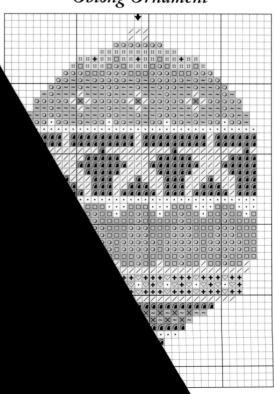

Round Ornament

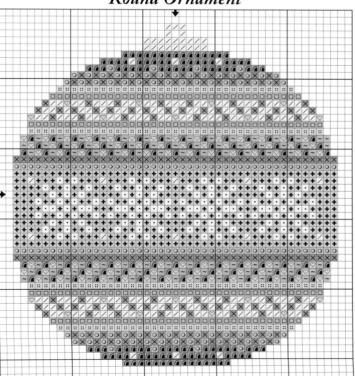

Star Light

Design by Cathy Bussi

Touches of metallic add richness to a design that is striking in its simplicity and sentiment!

Materials
- Bonnie blue 32-count linen: 15½ x 14½ inches
- Kreinik blending filament: silver #001 and gold #002

"Star Light" was stitched on Bonnie blue 32-count linen by Wichelt using DMC floss. Finished piece was custom framed.

Skill Level
**Average

Stitch Count
126 wide x 108 high

Approximate Design Size
11-count 11½" x 9⅞"
14-count 9" x 7¾"
16-count 7⅞" x 6¾"
18-count 7" x 6"
22-count 5¾" x 5"
32-count over two threads: 7⅞" x 6¾"

Instructions
1. Center and stitch design, stitching over two threads using two strands blending filament or floss, or two strands floss with one strand blending filament for Cross-Stitch, two strands floss and one strand blending filament for Eyelet Stitch and one strand of floss for Backstitch and French Knot (See Eyelet Stitch illustration on page 141.) ❖

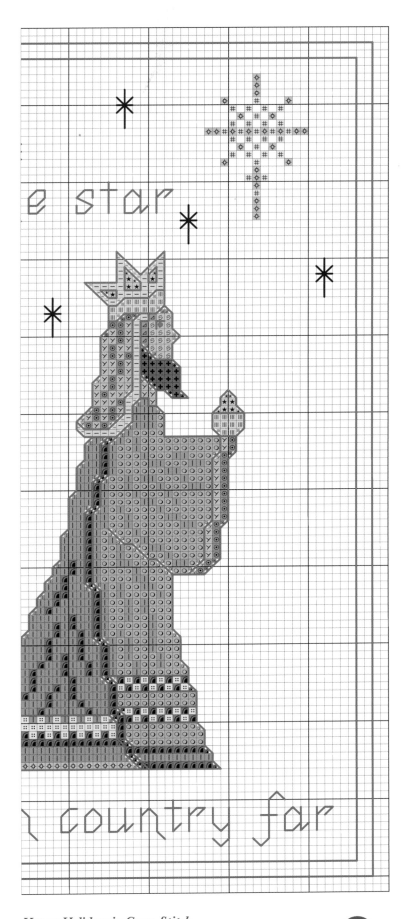

CROSS-STITCH (2X)

ANCHOR		DMC	COLORS
120	–	159	Light gray blue
939	Y	160	Medium gray blue
122	⊙	161	Gray blue
1025	◪	347	Very dark salmon
362	e	437	Light tan
878	••	501	Dark blue green
8581	⊠	646	Dark beaver gray
891	◢	676	Light old gold
890	∅	729	Medium old gold
361	□	738	Very light tan
234	✳	762	Very light pearl gray
1086	✚	839	Dark beige brown
1084	◢	840	Medium beige brown
1082	⑤	841	Light beige brown
4146	⋮	950	Light desert sand
1024	▌	3328	Dark salmon
1023	◯	3712	Medium salmon
1009	=	3773	Medium desert sand
877	↳	3815	Dark celadon green
876	◊	3816	Celadon green
1	•	B5200	Snow white
KREINIK BF			COLORS
001	★		Silver
002	☆		Gold

KREINIK BLENDED CROSS-STITCH

ANCHOR		DMC	COLORS
1	⌗	B5200	Snow white* (2X) with 001 silver BF (1X)
120	⠶	159	Light gray blue* (2X) with 001 silver BF* (1X)
121	⊕	160	Medium gray blue* (2X) with 001 silver BF* (1X)
398	∧	415	Pearl gray (2X) with 001 silver BF* (1X)
890	~	729	Medium old gold* (2X) with 002 gold BF* (1X)
234	⦀	762	Very light pearl gray* (2X) with 001 silver BF* (1X)
386	⊘	3823	Ultra pale yellow (2X) with 002 gold BF* (1X)

KREINIK BLENDED EYELET STITCH

ANCHOR		DMC	COLORS
1	➖	B5200	Snow white* (2X) with 001 silver BF* (1X) (small stars)

BACKSTITCH (1X)

ANCHOR		DMC	COLORS
122	—	161	Gray blue* (border)
150	—	336	Navy blue (lettering)
236	—	3799	Very dark pewter gray (all kings)

FRENCH KNOT (1X)

ANCHOR		DMC	COLORS
150	●	336	Navy blue*
236	●	3799	Very dark pewter gray* (eyes)

*Duplicate color

Christmas Sweeties

Design by Susan Pisoni,
Adapted for Cross-Stitch by Marilyn Frable

Stitch these sweet little characters on 14-count perforated plastic for long-lasting treats that you'll display year after year. Hint: they also make great package decorations!

Materials
- 14-count brown perforated plastic or paper: 1 sheet
- Kreinik blending filament: pearl #032
- Kreinik #8 fine braid: gold hi lustre #002HL
- 9 x 12-inch sheet tan felt
- Fabric adhesive

"Christmas Sweeties" were stitched using DMC floss.

Skill Level
**Average

Star
Stitch Count
46 wide x 47 high

Approximate Design Size
11-count 4⅛" x 4¼"
14-count 3¼" x 3⅜"
16-count 2⅞" x 3"
18-count 2½" x 2⅝"
22-count 2" x 2⅛"

Candy Cane
Stitch Count
36 wide x 48 high

Approximate Design Size
11-count 3¼" x 4⅜"
14-count 2½" x 3⅜"
16-count 2¼" x 3"
18-count 2" x 2⅝"
22-count 1⅝" x 2⅛"

Gingerbread Man
Stitch Count
36 wide x 48 high

Approximate Design Size
11-count 3¼" x 4⅜"
14-count 2½" x 3⅜"
16-count 2¼" x 3"

18-count 2" x 2⅝"
22-count 1⅝" x 2⅛"

Peppermint Stitch Count

46 wide x 48 high

Approximate Design Size

11-count 4⅛" x 4⅜"
14-count 3¼" x 3⅜"
16-count 2⅞" x 3"
18-count 2½" x 2⅝"
22-count 2" x 2⅛"

Christmas Tree Stitch Count

33 wide x 46 high

Approximate Design Size

11-count 3" x 4⅛"
14-count 2⅜" x 3¼"
16-count 2" x 2⅞"
18-count 1⅞" x 2¼"
22-count 1½" x 2"

Instructions

1. Leaving at least four holes between individual designs, stitch designs on brown perforated plastic or paper using two strands of floss, two strands of floss and one strand blending filament, or one strand fine braid for Cross-Stitch; and one or two strands floss or one strand fine braid for Straight Stitch and Backstitch. Work French Knot as indicated in key for each design.

Finishing

1. Trim plastic or paper one hole beyond stitching.

2. For each ornament, cut an 8-inch strand of fine braid; glue both ends to the top back of ornament to form a hanging loop.

3. Glue each ornament to felt; let dry. Trim felt to fit ornament. ❖

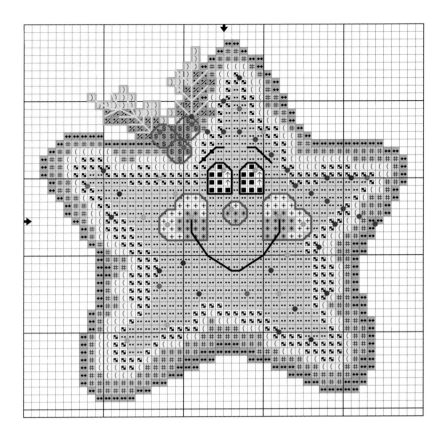

Star

CROSS-STITCH (2X)

ANCHOR		DMC	COLORS
2	↑	White	White
403	■	310	Black
1045	◆◆	436	Tan
362	#	437	Light tan
46	$	666	Bright red
228	⁄	700	Bright green
295	••	726	Light topaz
300	◪	745	Light pale yellow
275	(	746	Off white
203	)	954	Nile green
76	✳	961	Dark dusty rose
74	+	3354	Light dusty rose

BACKSTITCH (1X)

ANCHOR		DMC	COLORS
403	—	310	Black*
43	—	815	Medium garnet
203	═	954	Nile green*
236	═	3799	Very dark pewter gray

KREINIK BLENDED FRENCH KNOT

ANCHOR		DMC	COLORS
2	●	White	White* (1X) with 032 pearl BF (1X) (cheeks and eyes)
2	●	White	White* (2X) with 032 pearl BF* (1X)

FRENCH KNOT (2X)

ANCHOR		DMC	COLOR
403	●	310	Black* (cheeks)

FRENCH KNOT (3X)

ANCHOR		DMC	COLORS
2	●	White	White*
46	●	666	Bright red*
228	●	700	Bright green*
74	●	3354	Light dusty rose*

FRENCH KNOT (6X, 2-wrap)

ANCHOR		DMC	COLOR
1005	●	498	Dark red

*Duplicate color

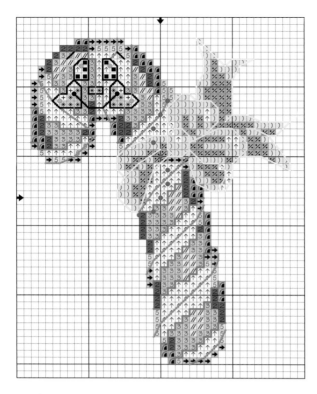

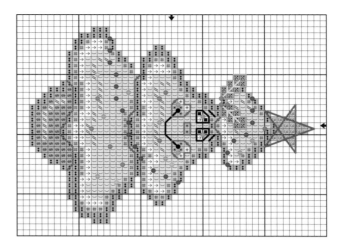

Candy Cane

CROSS-STITCH (2X)

ANCHOR		DMC	COLORS
2	↑	White	White
1006	3	304	Medium red
403	■	310	Black
235	→	414	Dark steel gray
1005	2	498	Dark red
228	⅔	700	Bright green
43	◪	815	Medium garnet
274	5	928	Very light gray green
203	)	954	Nile green
76	✳	961	Dark dusty rose
74	+	3354	Light dusty rose

KREINIK BLENDED CROSS-STITCH

ANCHOR		DMC	COLORS
2	⫽	White	White (2x) with 032 pearl BF (1x)

BACKSTITCH (1X)

ANCHOR		DMC	COLORS
403	—	310	Black*
43	—	815	Medium garnet*
236	—	3799	Very dark pewter gray

BACKSTITCH (2X)

ANCHOR		DMC	COLOR
46	—	666	Bright red

KREINIK BLENDED FRENCH KNOT

ANCHOR		DMC	COLORS
2	●	White	White* (1X) with 032 pearl BF* (1X) (eyes and cheeks)

FRENCH KNOT (2X)

ANCHOR		DMC	COLOR
403	●	310	Black*

FRENCH KNOT (6X, 2-wrap)

ANCHOR		DMC	COLOR
1005	●	498	Dark red*

*Duplicate color

Christmas Tree

CROSS-STITCH (2X)

ANCHOR		DMC	COLORS
2	↑	White	White
403	■	310	Black
1045	◆◆	436	Tan
362	#	437	Light tan
46	$	666	Bright red
228	⅔	700	Bright green
203	)	954	Nile green
76	✳	961	Dark dusty rose
74	+	3354	Light dusty rose

KREINIK BLENDED CROSS-STITCH

ANCHOR		DMC	COLORS
2	⫽	White	White* (2x) with 032 pearl BF (1x)

CROSS-STITCH (1X)

KREINIK #8 BRAID		COLOR
002HL	3	Gold high lustre

STRAIGHT STITCH (1X)

KREINIK #8 BRAID		COLOR
002HL	▬	Gold high lustre*

BACKSTITCH (2X)

ANCHOR		DMC	COLORS
403	—	310	Black*
358	—	433	Medium brown
43	—	815	Medium garnet
203	—	954	Nile green
236	—	3799	Very dark pewter gray

KREINIK BLENDED FRENCH KNOT

ANCHOR		DMC	COLORS
2	●	White	White* (1X) with 032 pearl BF (1X)
2	●	White	White* (2X) with 032 pearl BF* (1X)

FRENCH KNOT (2X)

ANCHOR		DMC	COLOR
403	●	310	Black*

FRENCH KNOT (3X)

ANCHOR		DMC	COLORS
46	●	666	Bright red*
295	●	726	Light topaz
74	●	3354	Light dusty rose*

FRENCH KNOT (6X, 2-wrap)

ANCHOR		DMC	COLOR
1005	●	498	Dark red

*Duplicate color

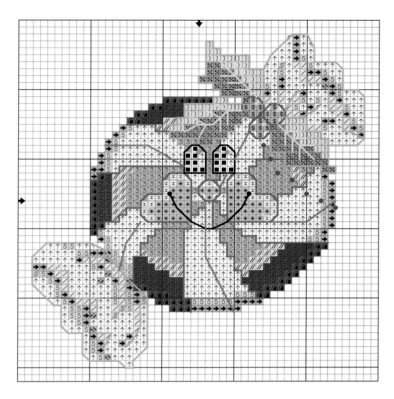

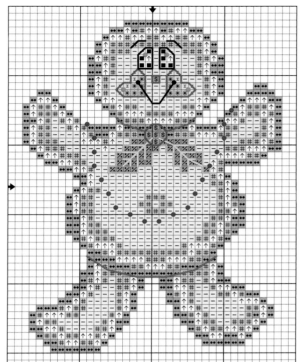

Peppermint

CROSS-STITCH (2X)

ANCHOR		DMC	COLORS
2	↑	White	White
1006	3	304	Medium red
403	■	310	Black
235	→	414	Dark steel gray
1005	2	498	Dark red
46	$	666	Bright red
228	%	700	Bright green
43	◣	815	Medium garnet
274	5	928	Very light gray green
203	)	954	Nile green
76	✳	961	Dark dusty rose
74	I	3354	Light dusty rose
236	∕	3799	Very dark pewter gray

KREINIK BLENDED CROSS-STITCH

ANCHOR		DMC	COLORS
2	∕∕	White	White* (1X) with 032 pearl BF (1X)

BACKSTITCH (1X)

ANCHOR		DMC	COLORS
403	━	310	Black*
43	━	815	Medium garnet*
203	═	954	Nile green*
236	═	3799	Very dark pewter gray*

BACKSTITCH (2X)

ANCHOR		DMC	COLOR
46	━	666	Bright red*

KREINIK BLENDED FRENCH KNOT

ANCHOR		DMC	COLORS
2	●	White	White* (1X) with 032 pearl BF* (1X)
2	○	White	White* (2X) with 032 pearl BF* (1X)

FRENCH KNOT (2X)

ANCHOR		DMC	COLOR
403	●	310	Black*

FRENCH KNOT (6X, 2-wrap)

ANCHOR		DMC	COLOR
1005	●	498	Dark red*

*Duplicate color

Gingerbread Man

CROSS-STITCH (2X)

ANCHOR		DMC	COLORS
2	↑	White	White
403	■	310	Black
1045	◆◆	436	Tan
362	#	437	Light tan
46	$	666	Bright red
228	%	700	Bright green
387	−	739	Ultra very light tan
76	✳	961	Dark dusty rose
74	I	3354	Light dusty rose

BACKSTITCH (1X)

ANCHOR		DMC	COLORS
403	━	310	Black*
358	━	433	Medium brown
43	━	815	Medium garnet
203	═	954	Nile green*
236	═	3799	Very dark pewter gray

KREINIK BLENDED FRENCH KNOT

ANCHOR		DMC	COLOR
2	●	White	White* (1X) with 032 pearl BF (1X)

FRENCH KNOT (2X)

ANCHOR		DMC	COLOR
403	●	310	Black*

FRENCH KNOT (6X, 2-wrap)

ANCHOR		DMC	COLOR
1005	●	498	Dark red

*Duplicate color

Midnight Santa

Design by Patty Cox

A man-in-the-moon Santa will reaffirm your belief in the wonder and magic of the holidays!

CROSS-STITCH (2X)

ANCHOR		DMC	COLORS
9046	✖	321	Red
9	↑	352	Light coral
923	✔	699	Green
228	)	700	Bright green
1012	$	754	Light peach
43	♥	815	Medium garnet
1034	0	931	Medium antique blue
1011	4	948	Very light peach
1031	m	3753	Ultra very light antique blue

CROSS-STITCH (1X)

KREINIK #8 BRAID		COLOR
	C	001	Silver

BACKSTITCH (1X)

ANCHOR		DMC	COLOR
403	—	310	Black

Materials

- Opalescent 14-count Aida: 9 x 9 inches
- Kreinik #8 fine braid: silver #001

"Midnight Santa" was stitched on Aida by Zweigart using DMC floss.

Skill Level

**Average

Stitch Count

47 wide x 49 high

Approximate Design Size

11-count 4⅜" x 4½"
14-count 3⅜" x 3½"
16-count 3" x 3⅛"
18-count 2⅝" x 2¾"
22-count 2⅛" x 2¼"

Instructions

1. Center and stitch design using two strands floss or one strand fine braid for Cross-Stitch and one strand floss for Backstitch. ❖

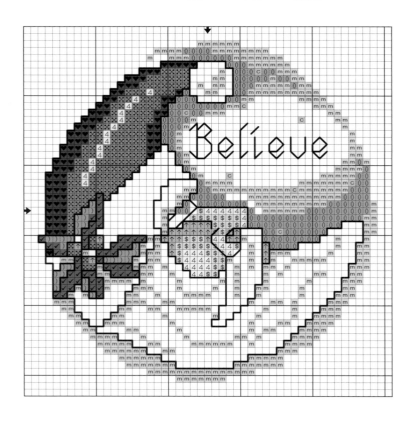

Design by Mike Vickery

With candy-striped turrets and gift-box windows, this castle is fit for the most famous of all Christmas characters—Santa himself!

Materials

- White 14-count Aida: 14 x 18 inches

"Santa's Castle" was stitched on white 14-count Aida by Zweigart using DMC floss. Finished piece was custom framed.

Skill Level

**Average

Stitch Count

112 wide x 179 high

Approximate Design Size

11-count 10⅛" x 16¼"
14-count 8" x 12¾"
16-count 7" x 11⅛"
18-count 6¼" x 10"
22-count 5" x 8⅛"

Instructions

1. Center and stitch design on 14-count Aida, using three strands floss for Cross-Stitch and one strand floss for Backstitch. ❖

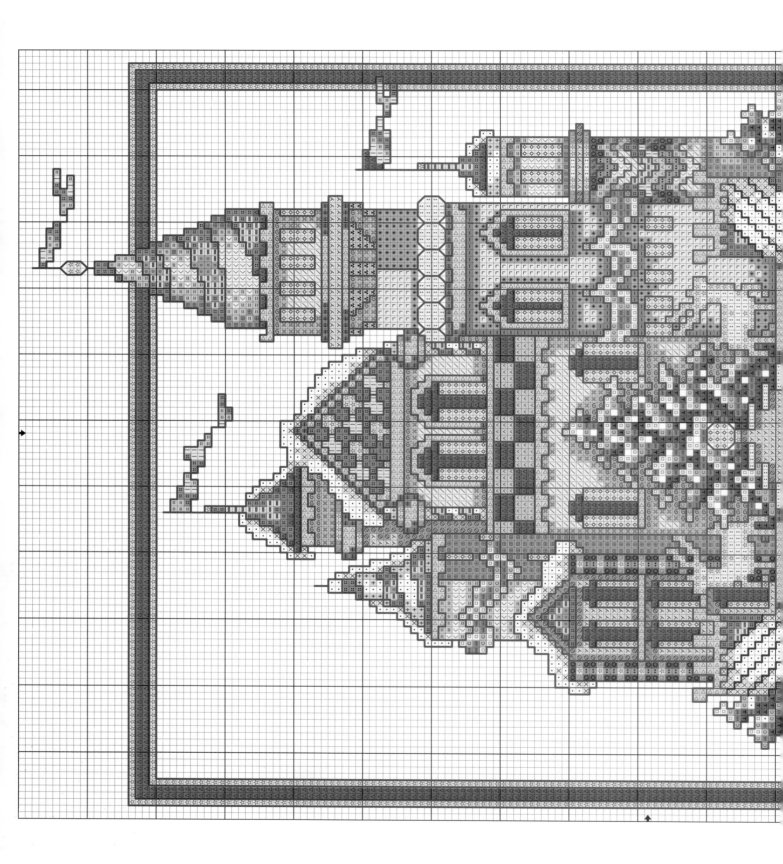

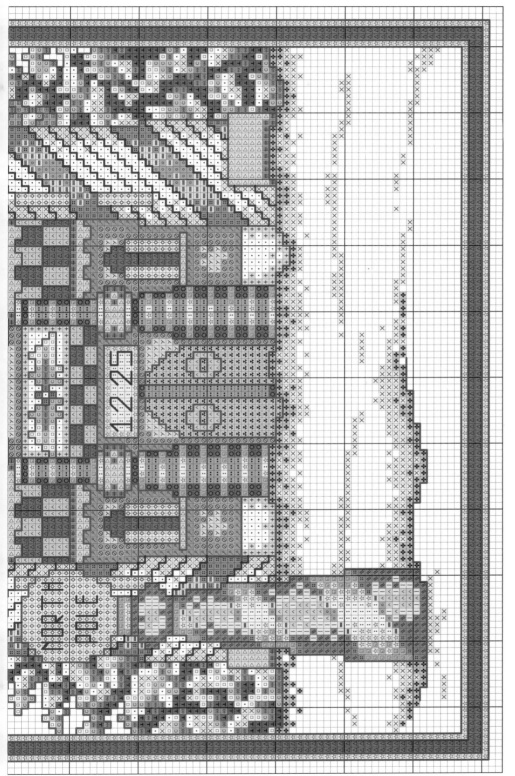

CROSS-STITCH (3X)

ANCHOR		DMC	COLORS
2	·	White	White
218	⊥	319	Very dark pistachio green
215	⋘	320	Medium pistachio green
9046	∷	321	Red
261	C	368	Light pistachio green
1043	▢	369	Very light pistachio green
1046	▼	435	Very light brown
1005	△	498	Dark red
891	⊡	676	Light old gold
886	☆	677	Very light old gold
305	=	725	Medium light topaz
293	<	727	Very light topaz
275	∶	746	Off-white
158	╱	747	Very light sky blue
128	✕	775	Very light baby blue
308	⊞	782	Dark topaz
168	↻	807	Peacock blue
390	+	822	Light beige gray
229	⇗	910	Dark emerald green
209	Ι	912	Light emerald green
850	∅	926	Medium gray green
274	Y	928	Very light gray green
203	∧	954	Nile green
871	⧻	3041	Medium antique violet
870	▷	3042	Light antique violet
129	✦	3325	Light baby blue
68	✿	3687	Mauve
66	••	3688	Medium mauve
33	○	3706	Medium melon
167	⌘	3766	Light peacock blue
779	⋌	3768	Dark gray green
35	=	3801	Very dark melon
216	–	3815	Dark celadon green
215	✳	3816	Celadon green
213	⌐	3817	Light celadon green
275	⊹	3823	Ultra pale yellow

BACKSTITCH (1X)

ANCHOR		DMC	COLORS
1005	▬	498	Dark red*
236	▬	3799	Very dark pewter gray

*Duplicate color

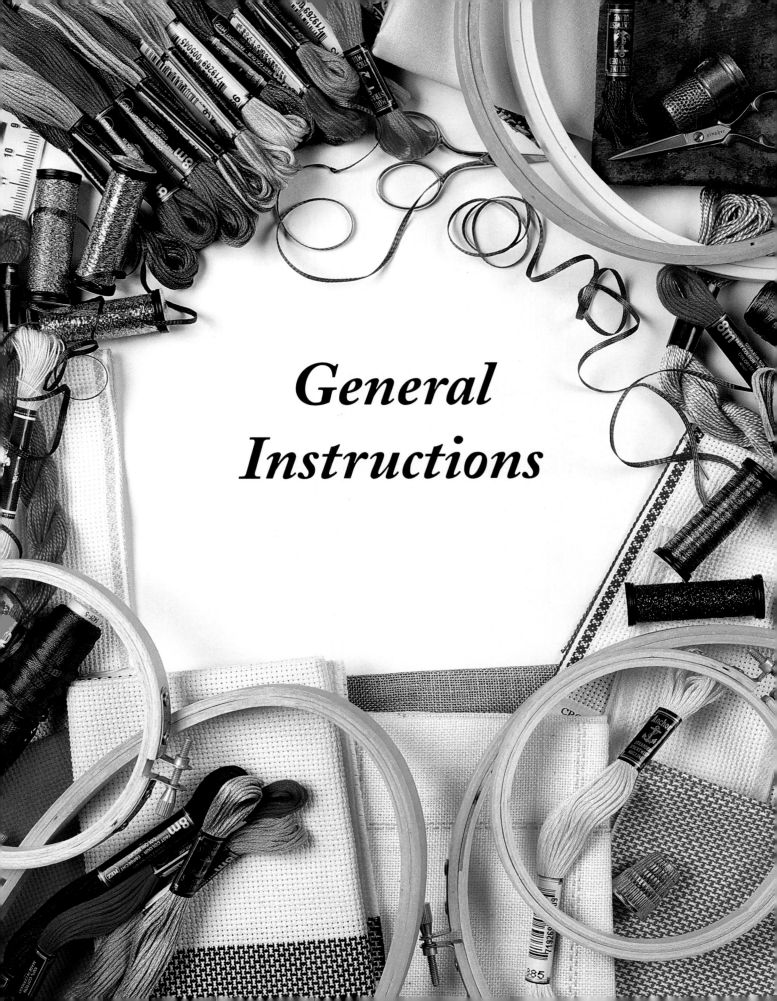

General Instructions

Tools of the Stitcher

Fabrics

Most counted cross-stitch projects are worked on evenweave fabrics made especially for counted thread embroidery. These fabrics have vertical and horizontal threads of uniform thickness and spacing. Aida cloth is a favorite of beginning stitchers because its weave forms distinctive squares in the fabric, which makes placing stitches easy. To determine a fabric's thread count, count the number of threads per inch of fabric.

Linen is made from fibers of the flax plant and is strong and durable. Its lasting quality makes it the perfect choice for heirloom projects. Linen is available in a range of muted colors and stitch counts.

In addition to evenweave fabrics, many stitchers enjoy using waste canvas and perforated paper. Waste canvas is basted to clothing or other fabric, forming a grid for stitching which is later removed. Perforated paper has holes evenly spaced for 14 stitches per inch.

Needles

Cross-stitch needles should have elongated eyes and blunt points. They should slip easily between the threads of the fabric, but should not pierce the fabric. The most common sizes used for cross-stitching are size 24 or 26. The ideal needle size is just small enough to slip easily through your fabric. Some stitchers prefer to use a slightly smaller needle for backstitching. When stitching on waste canvas, use a sharp needle.

Hoops, Frames & Scissors

Hoops can be round or oval and come in many sizes. The three main types are plastic, spring-tension and wooden. Frames are easier on the fabric than hoops and come in many sizes and shapes. Once fabric is mounted it doesn't have to be removed until stitching is complete, saving fabric from excessive handling.

Small, sharp scissors are essential for cutting floss and removing mistakes. For cutting fabrics, invest in a top-quality pair of medium-sized sewing scissors. To keep them in top form, use these scissors only for cutting fabrics and floss.

Stitching Threads

Today's cross-stitcher can achieve a vast array of effects in texture, color and shine. In addition to the perennial favorite, six-strand floss, stitchers can choose from sparkling metallics, shiny rayons, silks, narrow ribbon threads and much more.

Six-Strand Floss

Six-strand floss comes in a variety of colors and is available in metallics, silk and rayon as well as cotton. Most projects are worked using two or three strands of floss for cross-stitches and one or two strands for backstitches. For ease of stitching and to prevent wear on fibers, use lengths no longer than 18 inches.

Pearl Cotton

Pearl cotton is available in #3, #5, #8 and #12, with #3 being the thickest. The plies of pearl cotton will not separate, and for most stitching one strand is used. Pearl cotton has a lustrous sheen.

Flower & Ribbon Threads

Flower thread has a tight twist and comes in many soft colors. It is heavier than one ply of six-strand floss—one strand of flower thread equals two strands of floss. Ribbon thread is a narrow ribbon especially created for stitching. It comes in a large number of colors in satin as well as metallic finishes.

Blending Filament & Metallic Braid

Blending filament is a fine, shiny fiber that can be used alone or combined with floss or other thread. Knotting the blending filament on the needle with a slipknot is recommended for control.

Metallic braid is a braided metallic fiber, usually used single-ply. Thread this fiber just as you would any other fiber. Use short lengths, about 15 inches, to keep the fiber from fraying.

Stitching With Beads

Small seed beads can be added to any cross-stitch design, using one bead per stitch. Knot thread at beginning of beaded section

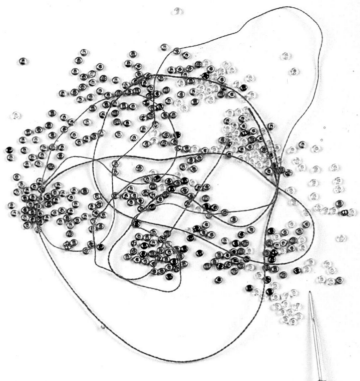

for security, especially if you are adding beads to clothing. The bead should lie in the same direction as the top half of cross-stitches.

Bead Attachment

Use one strand floss to secure beads. Bring beading needle up from back of work, leaving 2 inches length of thread hanging; do not knot (end will be secured between stitches as you work). Thread bead on needle; complete stitch.

Do not skip over more than two stitches or spaces without first securing thread, or last bead will be loose. To secure, weave thread into several stitches on back of work. Follow graph to work design, using one bead per stitch.

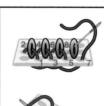

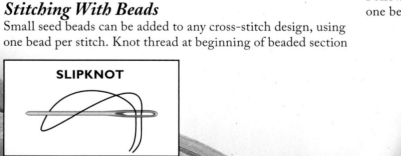

SLIPKNOT

Before You Begin

Assemble fabric, floss, pattern and tools. Familiarize yourself with the graph, color key and instructions before beginning.

Preparing Fabric

Before you stitch, decide how large to cut fabric. If you are making a pillow or other design which requires a large unstitched area, be sure to leave plenty of fabric. If you are making a small project, leave at least 3 inches around all edges of design. Determine the design area size by using this formula: number of stitches across design area divided by the number of threads per inch of fabric equals size of fabric in inches. Measure fabric, then cut evenly along horizontal and vertical threads.

Press out folds. To prevent raveling, hand overcast or machine zigzag fabric edges. Find center of fabric by folding horizontally and vertically, and mark with a small stitch.

Reading Graphs

Cross-stitch graphs or charts are made up of colors and symbols to tell you the exact color, type and placement of each stitch. Each square represents the area for one complete cross-stitch. Next to each graph, there is a key with information about stitches and floss colors represented by the graph's colors and symbols.

Some graphs are so large they must be divided for printing.

Preparing Floss

The six strands of floss are easily separated, and the number of strands used is given in instructions. Cut strands in 14–18 inches lengths. When separating floss, always separate all six strands, then recombine the number of strands needed. To make floss separating easier, run cut length across a damp sponge. To prevent floss from tangling, run cut length through a fabric-softener dryer sheet before separating and threading needle. To colorfast red floss tones, which sometimes bleed, hold floss under running water until water runs clear. Allow to air dry.

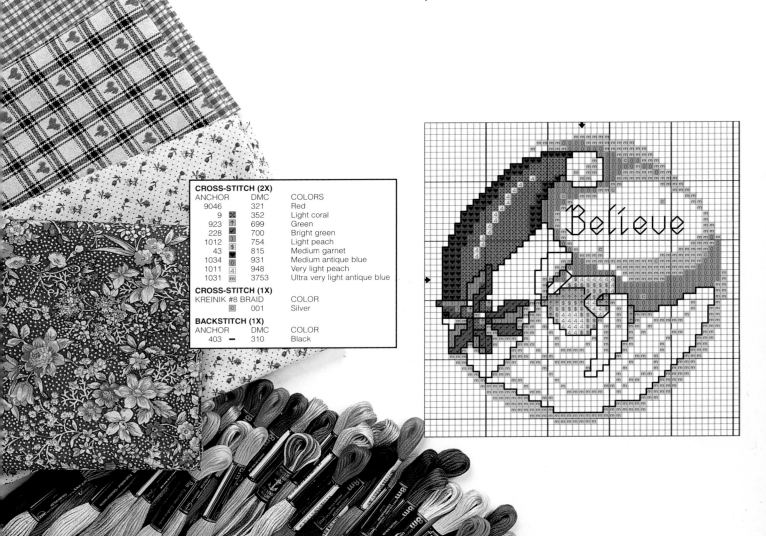

CROSS-STITCH (2X)

ANCHOR		DMC	COLORS
9046		321	Red
9	▒	352	Light coral
923	↑	699	Green
228	✔	700	Bright green
1012	⟩	754	Light peach
43	■	815	Medium garnet
1034	0	931	Medium antique blue
1011	4	948	Very light peach
1031	m	3753	Ultra very light antique blue

CROSS-STITCH (1X)

KREINIK #8 BRAID		COLOR
	c	001	Silver

BACKSTITCH (1X)

ANCHOR		DMC	COLOR
403	—	310	Black

Stitching Techniques

Beginning & Ending a Thread

Try these methods for beginning a thread, then decide which one is best for you.

Securing the thread: Start by pulling needle through fabric back to front, leaving about 1 inch behind fabric. Hold this end with fingers as you begin stitching, and work over end with your first few stitches. After work is in progress, weave end through the back of a few stitches.

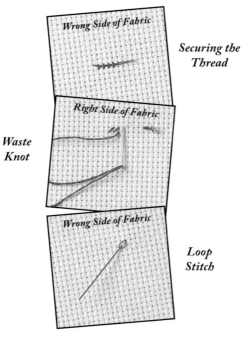

Waste knot: Make a knot in end of floss and pull needle through fabric front to back several squares over from where your first cross-stitch will be. Come up at first stitch and stitch first few stitches over floss end. Clip knot.

Loop stitch: This method can only be used for even numbers of strands. Cut strands twice the normal length, then take half the number of strands needed and fold in half. Insert loose ends in needle and bring needle up from back at first stitch, leaving loop underneath. Take needle down through fabric and through loop; pull to secure.

For even stitches, keep a consistent tension on your thread, and pull thread and needle completely through fabric with each stab of the needle. Make all the top crosses on your cross-stitches face the same direction. To finish a thread, run the needle under the back side of several stitches and clip. Threads carried across the back of unworked areas may show through to the front, so do not carry threads.

Master Stitchery

Work will be neater if you always try to make each stitch by coming up in an unoccupied hole and going down in an occupied hole.

The sewing method is preferred for stitching on linen and some other evenweaves, but can also be used on Aida. Stitches are made as in hand-sewing with needle going from front to back to front of fabric in one motion. All work is done from the front of the fabric. When stitching with the sewing method, it is important not to pull thread too tightly or stitches will become distorted. Stitching on linen is prettiest with the sewing method, using no hoop. If you use a hoop or frame when using the sewing method with Aida, keep in mind that fabric cannot be pulled taut. There must be "give" in the fabric in order for needle to slip in and out easily.

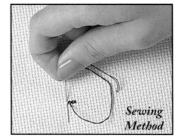

In the stab method, needle and floss are taken completely through fabric twice with each stitch. For the first half of the stitch, bring needle up and pull thread completely through fabric to the front. Then take needle down and reach underneath and pull completely through to bottom.

Working on Evenweave

When working on linen or other evenweave fabric, keep needle on right side of fabric, taking needle front to back to front with each stitch. Work over two threads, placing the beginning and end of the bottom half of the first cross-stitch where a vertical thread crosses a horizontal thread.

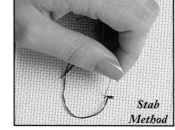

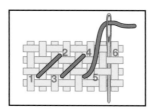

Cleaning Your Needlework

Careful washing, pressing and sometimes blocking help preserve and protect your stitched piece. After stitching is complete, a gentle washing will remove surface dirt, hoop marks and hand oils that have accumulated on your fabric while stitching. Even if a piece looks clean, it's always a good idea to give it a nice cleaning before finishing. Never press your work before cleaning, as this only serves to set those hoop marks and soils that are best removed.

Using a gentle soap such as baby shampoo or gentle white dishwashing liquid and a large, clean bowl, make a solution of cool, sudsy water. If you use a hand-wash product, make sure the one you choose contains no chlorine bleach. Fill another bowl or sink with plain cool water for rinsing.

Soak your stitched piece in sudsy water for five to ten minutes. Then gently and without rubbing or twisting, squeeze suds through fabric several times. Dip piece several times in fresh, cool water, until no suds remain.

On rare occasions floss colors will run or fade slightly. When this happens, continue to rinse in cool water until water becomes perfectly clear. Remove fabric from water and lay on a soft, white towel. Never twist or wring your work. Blot excess water away and roll the piece up in the towel, pressing gently.

Never allow a freshly washed piece of embroidery to air dry. Instead, remove the damp piece from the towel and place face down on a fresh, dry white towel. To prevent color stains, it's important to keep the stitched piece flat, not allowing stitched areas to touch each other or other areas of the fabric. Make sure the edges of fabric are in straight lines and even. To be sure fabric edges are straight when pressing dry, use a ruler or T-square to check edges. Wash towel several times before using it to block cross-stitch, and use it only for this purpose.

After edges are aligned and fabric is perfectly smooth, cover the back of the stitched piece with a pressing cloth, cotton diaper or other lightweight white cotton cloth. Press dry with a dry iron set on a high permanent press or cotton setting, depending on fabric content. Allow stitchery to lie in this position several hours. Machine-drying is acceptable after use for items like towels and kitchen accessories, but your work will be prettier and smoother if you give these items a careful pressing the first time.

Framing and Mounting

Shopping for Frames

When you shop for a frame, take the stitchery along with you and compare several frame and mat styles. Keep in mind the "feeling" of your stitched piece when choosing a frame. For example, an exquisite damask piece stitched with metallics and silk threads might need an ornate gold frame, while a primitive sampler stitched on dirty linen with flower thread would need a simpler, perhaps wooden frame.

Mounting

Cross-stitch pieces can be mounted on mat board, white cardboard, special padded or unpadded mounting boards designed specifically for needlework, or special acid-free mat board available from art-supply stores. Acid-free framing materials are the best choice for projects you wish to keep well-preserved for future generations. If you prefer a padded look, cut quilt batting to fit mounting board.

Center blocked stitchery over mounting board of choice with quilt batting between, if desired. Leaving 1½ to 3 inches around all edges, trim excess fabric away along straight of grain.

Mounting boards made for needlework have self-stick surfaces and require no pins. When using these products, lift and smooth needlework onto board until work is taut and edges are smooth and even. Turn board face down and smooth fabric to back, mitering corners.

Pins are required for other mounting boards. With design face up, keeping fabric straight and taut, insert a pin through fabric and edge of mounting board at the center of each side. Turn piece face down and smooth excess fabric to back, mitering corners.

There are several methods for securing fabric edges. Edges may be glued to mat board with liquid fabric glue or fabric glue stick. If mat board is thick, fabric may be stapled.

Mats & Glass

Precut mats are available in many sizes and colors to fit standard-size frames. Custom mats are available in an even wider variety of colors, textures and materials. Using glass over cross-stitch is a matter of personal preference, but is generally discouraged. Moisture can collect behind glass and rest on fabric, causing mildew stains. A single or double mat will hold glass away from fabric.

Stitch Guide

Basic Stitchery

Cross-Stitch: There are two ways of making a basic Cross-Stitch. The first method is used when working rows of stitches in the same color. The first step makes the bottom half of the stitches across the row, and the second step makes the top half.

The second method is used when making single stitches. The bottom and top halves of each stitch are worked before starting the next stitch.

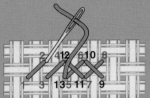

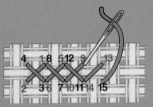

Quarter Cross-Stitch: Stitch may slant in any direction.

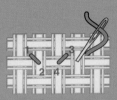

Three-Quarter Cross-Stitch A Half Cross-Stitch plus a Quarter Cross-Stitch may slant in any direction.

Half Cross-Stitch: The first part of a Cross-Stitch may slant in either direction.

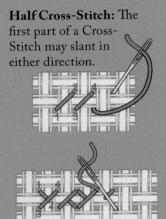

Embellishing With Embroidery

EMBROIDERY stitches add detail and dimension to stitching. Unless otherwise noted, work Backstitches first, then other embroidery stitches.

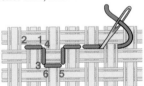

Backstitch

French Knot

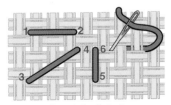

Straight Stitch

Special Stitches

Modified Eyelet Stitch

Eyelet Stitch

Double Cross-Stitch

Herringbone Stitch

Cross-Stitch Supplies

Page 6: Dance Hall Revue
• Lady blue 14-count Aida by Zweigart
• Blending filament by Kreinik Mfg. Co. Inc.

Page 12: January Sampler
• Ice blue 28-count Cashel Linen by Zweigart
• #4 very fine braid by Kreinik Mfg. Co. Inc.
• Beads and snowflake charm #12039 by Mill Hill

Page 14: Winter's Eve
• White 14-count Aida by Wichelt Imports Inc.

Page 16: Snowflake Coasters
• Antique blue 14-count Aida by Charles Craft Inc. Inc.

Page 18: Winter Visitor
• Light blue 28-count Jobelan by Wichelt Imports Inc.
• #4 very fine braid by Kreinik Mfg. Co. Inc.

Page 21: God Is Love
• Water lily 28-count Linen by Wichelt Imports Inc.
• Silk Mori Milk Paint and #4 very fine braid by Kreinik Mfg. Co. Inc.
• Glass beads by Mill Hill
• Ecru #8 Pearl Cotton by DMC Corp.

Page 24: February Sampler
• Ice carnation 28-count Cashel Linen by Zweigart
• #4 very fine braid by Kreinik Mfg. Co. Inc.
• Beads and heart charm #12207 by Mill Hill

Page 26: Sewing Bees
• White 28-count Linen by Zweigart
• #4 very fine braid and Japan thread by Kreinik Mfg. Co. Inc.
• Oval Shaker Box #99671, Oval Pincushion #99651 and Key Rack #10168 by Sudberry House
• Beads and treasure by Mill Hill

Page 32: Hearts and Flowers
• Antique white 14-count Aida by Wichelt Imports Inc.
• Blending filament by Kreinik Mfg. Co. Inc.

Page 35: Irish Blessing
• White 14-count Aida by Zweigart
• Coaster/Candydish #15801 by Sudberry House

Page 36: March Sampler
• Mint green 28-count Cashel Linen by Zweigart
• #4 very fine braid by Kreinik Mfg. Co. Inc.
• Beads and shamrock charm #12145 by Mill Hill

Page 38: Celtic Sachets
• Apricot, carnation pink and mint green 28-count Cashel Linen by Zweigart
• Eterna Silk floss by Yodamo Inc.

Page 40: Easter Memories
• Baby lotion 28-count Lugana by Zweigart

Page 42: Easter Eggs
• #4 very fine braid and #8 fine braid by Kreinik Mfg. Co. Inc.

Page 44: Happy Easter
• Miracle mint 25-count Lugana by Zweigart

Page 46: Spring Easter Egg
• Victorian blue 14-count Aida by Zweigart

Page 47: Wildflower Bouquet
• Rondo tablecloth #2447/1 and Champagne napkin #1960/1 white by Zweigart

Page 50: Topiary Trio
• Ivory 14-count Aida by Wichelt Imports Inc.

Page 54: Morning Glory Mini Purse
• White 14-count Crafter's Pride Vinyl-Weave by Daniel Enterprises
• #8 fine braid by Kreinik Mfg. Co. Inc.

Page 57: The Hunter and the Yei
• Antique white 14-count Aida by Wichelt Imports Inc.
• Blending filament by Kreinik Mfg. Co. Inc.

Page 60: Par Four Desk Accessories
• White 18-count Aida by DMC Corp.

Page 62: Little Treasure Clock
• Daffodil 22-count Softana by Zweigart
• Little Treasure Clock #48241 by Sudberry House

Page 66: Hurrah!
• Antique white 28-count Cashel Linen by Zweigart

Page 68: Only When It's Dark
• Navy blue 14-count Aida by Zweigart

Page 70: God Bless America
• White 14-count Aida by Zweigart

Page 73: Birthday Bears
• #4 very fine braid by Kreinik Mfg. Co. Inc.
• January—Barely blue 28-count Jobelan by Wichelt Imports Inc.
• January—Blue small moiré box #99762 by Sudberry House
• February—Crafter's Pride black address book #30710 available from Daniel Enterprises
• March—Crafter's Pride tissue box cover #20900, available from Daniel Enterprises
• April—Buttermilk 28-count Jobelan by Wichelt Imports Inc.
• May—Antique white 14-count Lady Elizabeth pillow sham #PS-7780-0322 by Charles Craft Inc.
• June—Honey suckle pink 28-count Jobelan by Wichelt Imports Inc.

- June—7½-inch Teddy bear fabric holder #67317 by Ackfeld Manufacturing
- July—White 14-count Showcase huck towel #HF-6500-6750-EA by Charles Craft Inc.
- August—Cameo peach 28-count Jobelan by Wichelt Imports Inc.
- September—White 14-count Aida place mat #RC-4851-6750-PK by Charles Craft Inc.
- October—Water lily 28-count Jobelan by Wichelt Imports Inc.
- November—Crafter's Pride Trivet #TR01 available from Daniel Enterprises
- December—Delicate teal 28-count Jobelan by Wichelt Imports Inc.
- December—Narrow gold mirror #2209G by Sudberry House

Page 89: Happy Hauntings
- Café mocha 32-count Country French Linen by Wichelt Imports Inc.
- Blending filament by Kreinik Mfg. Co. Inc.

Page 92: Happy Halloween
- Crafter's Pride Milano Waffle Weave Towel #11730 by Daniel Enterprises

Page 94: Boo! Tote
- Buttons: ghost #86024, witch #86025, bat #86026, trick or treat boy #86032B, trick or treat girl #86032G and trick or treat pumpkin #86033 by Mill Hill

Page 96: Horn of Plenty
- Ivory 14-count Aida by Zweigart

Page 100: Be Thou Thankful
- Beige 14-count Aida by Charles Craft Inc.
- Hand over-dyed floss by Weeks Dye Works

Page 102: Thanksgiving Decor
- White 14-count place mat #RC-4851-6750 and white 14-count napkin #RC-4852-6750 by Charles Craft Inc. Inc.

Page 104: Holiday Duo
- Ecru showcase huck towel #HF-6500-2724-EA by Charles Craft
- Ecru kitchen mate pot holder #PH-6201-2724-EA by Charles Craft Inc.

Page 107: Santa's Cup of Tea
- Flax 32-count Belfast Linen by Zweigart
- Simply square box #99731 by Sudberry House

Page 110: Christmas Goodies Bellpull
- #8 fine braid by Kreinik Mfg. Co. Inc.

Page 112: Holiday Helper
- White showcase huck towel #HF-6500-6750-EA by Charles Craft Inc.

Page 114: Country Charm Ornament Bags
- Raw Linen 22-count Stitchband #7272/053 by Zweigart

Page 116: Snowman and Friends
- Natural 10-count Heatherfield by Wichelt Imports Inc.
- Penguin button #86146 and Cardinal button #86175 by Mill Hill

Page 117: Santa Sampler
- Antique white 14-count Aida by Zweigart

Page 120: Jewel-Tone Ornaments
- #4 very fine braid and #8 fine braid by Kreinik Mfg. Co. Inc.

Page 123: Star Light
- Bonnie blue 32-count Linen by Wichelt Imports Inc.
- Blending filament by Kreinik Mfg. Co. Inc.

Page 126: Christmas Sweeties
- Blending filament and #8 fine braid by Kreinik Mfg. Co. Inc.

Page 130: Midnight Santa
- Opalescent 14-count Aida by Zweigart
- #8 fine braid by Kreinik Mfg. Co. Inc.

Page 131: Santa's Castle
- White 14-count Aida by Zweigart

Cross-Stitch Sources

The following companies provided fabric and/or supplies for projects in this book. If you are unable to locate a product locally, contact the manufacturers listed below for the closest retail or mail-order source in your area.

Ackfeld Manufacturing
(417) 272-3135
www.ackfeldwire.com

Anchor Floss
Coats & Clark
(800) 648-1479
www.coatsandclark.com

Charles Craft Inc.
(800) 277-0980
www.charlescraft.com

Daniel Enterprises
(800) 277-6850
www.crafterspride.com

DMC Corp.
(937) 589-0606
www.dmc-usa.com

Mill Hill
www.millhillbeads.com

Kreinik Mfg. Co. Inc.
(410) 281-0040
www.kreinik.com

Olde Colonial Designs
(781) 834-8836

Sudberry House
(860) 739-6951
www.sudberry.com

The Gentle Art
(614) 855-8346
www.thegentleart.com

Weeks Dye Works
(877) 683-7393
www.weeksdyeworks.com

Wichelt Imports Inc.
(800) 356-9516
www.wichelt.com

Zweigart
(732) 562-8888
www.zweigart.com

Special Thanks

We would like to thank the talented cross-stitch designers whose work is featured in this collection.

C.M. Barr
Easter Memories, 40

Cathy Bussi
Star Light, 123

Gail Bussi
Hurrah!, 66
Happy Hauntings, 89
Santa's Cup of Tea, 107

Patti Cox
Midnight Santa, 130

Elaine Fuller
Little Treasure Clock, 62

Jackie Harris
Only When It's Dark, 68

Kathleen Hurley
Wildflower Bouquet, 47

Mary Jones
Snowflakes Coasters, 16

Pamela Kellogg
Birthday Bears, 73
February Sampler, 24
Hearts and Flowers, 32
Horn of Plenty, 96
January Sampler, 12
March Sampler, 36
Winter Visitor, 18

Carolyn Manning
Boo! Tote, 94

Patricia Maloney Martin
Halloween Hangers, 86
Irish Blessing, 35

Ursula Michaels
God Bless America, 70
Holiday Duo, 104
Holiday Helper, 112
Sewing Bees, 26

Hope Murphy
Country Charm Ornament
    Bags, 114

Susan Pisoni
Christmas Sweeties, 126
Dance Hall Revue, 6
Topiary Trio, 50

Roberta Rankin
Winter's Eve, 14

Carole Rodgers
Snowman and Friends, 116

Vicki Schofield
God Is Love, 21

Barbara Sestok
Happy Easter, 44

Susan Stadler
Be Thou Thankful, 100
Celtic Sachets, 38
The Hunter and the Yei, 57

Nancy Taylor
Roosters on Parade, 63
Spring Easter Egg, 46

Mike Vickery
Easter Eggs, 42
Par Four Desk Accessories, 60
Santa's Castle, 131

Lois Winston
Christmas Goodies Bellpull, 110
Happy Halloween, 92
Jewel-Tone Ornaments, 120
Santa Sampler, 117
Thanksgiving Decor, 102

Kathy Wirth
Morning Glory Mini Purse, 54